THE RETURN OF THE
WOLF

by
STEVE GROOMS

NorthWord
PRESS, INC

BOX 1360, MINOCQUA, WI 54548

Library of Congress Cataloging-in-Publication Data
Grooms, Steve
      The return of the wolf / by Steve Grooms.
         p. cm. -- (Camp & cottage series)
      ISBN 1-55971-151-5 : $16.95
      1. Wolves.   I. Title.   II. Series.
QL737.C22G76   1993
599.74'442--dc20   92-46208
                                         CIP

Front Cover designed by Russ Kuepper
Back cover, book interior, and maps designed by Kirstie Larsen
Edited by Greg Linder
ISBN 1-55971-151-5

Printed and bound in Hong Kong.

© 1993 Steve Grooms
Published by:
    NORTHWORD PRESS, INC.
    P.O. Box 1360
    Minocqua, WI 54548

For a free catalog describing NORTHWORD'S line of nature books and gifts, call 1-800-336-5666.

NORTHWORD'S "Camp and Cottage" series also includes:
    Bluebirds! by Steve Grooms and Dick Peterson
    The Great Blue Heron by Hayward Allen
    The Cry of the Sandhill Crane by Steve Grooms

DEDICATION

This book is for Molly, my favorite daughter and wolf research librarian. Thanks for the help and never quit caring about wolves.

ACKNOWLEDGMENTS

Perhaps the most appropriate way to begin this book is with a disclaimer. I'm a writer, not a wolf expert. Anything I know about wolves has been learned from people who have spent many years with wolves. In the course of researching this book, I spent a considerable amount of time talking with wolf researchers and managers. Without exception, they did their best to give intelligent answers to questions that were sometimes less than intelligent. Obviously, any mistakes in this text are mine and not the fault of all the people who tried to set me straight.

I've tried to keep track of the names. My sincere thanks go to Frankie Barker, Bill Berg, Vivian Bianci, Dick Bishop, Tony Booth, Bob Cary, Molly Clayton, Carol Cochran, Susan Cook, Gary Donovan, Hank Fischer, Steve Fritts, Dale Hagstrom, Jim Hammill, Cathie Harms, Art Hawkins, Carroll Henderson, Gary Henry, Henry Hilton, Evan Hirsche, Bobbie Holaday, Stephen Kuntz, Thomas Meyer, Michael Nelson, Alice Neve, Brian O'Neill, Mary Ortiz, Dave Parsons, Bill Paul, John Pierce, Walt Rohl, Dave Schad, Lori Schmidt, Peter Siminski, Bob Stephenson, Hans Stuart, Tom Talasz, Dick Thiel, Vick Van Ballenberghe, Adrian Wydeven, and Bruce Zoellick. For all his patience, special thanks go to Dan Groebner. My editor, Greg Linder, deserves credit for encouraging me to make the best wolf book possible, even if that meant using more words and time than I was supposed to.

Because the wolf is so controversial, it's inevitable that some people or groups will object to parts of this book. If they complain that I have failed to present all the relevant aspects of some argument, I will surely agree. The story of the wolf's return in this country is entirely too complicated to be covered in one book. An appendix lists a number of excellent wolf books for readers who wish to learn more about this fascinating animal.

CONTENTS

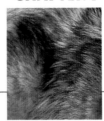

CHAPTER 1

Introduction

February is cold in the high Rockies, but wolves are well suited for bitter weather. A solitary young male, coal black and slightly large for his age, trots south through a mountain pass. His breath makes silvery vapor clouds that shimmer briefly in the moonlight. He notices nothing special as he passes out of British Columbia into the United States.

Where will he go?

If he turns east, this wolf will probably enter Glacier Park. Glacier was empty of wolves for half a century, but today four packs exploit the park's generous population of mule deer. A new wolf arriving in Glacier might have to deal with the aggression of the resident packs.

If he travels south for about three days, the young male will come to Montana's Ninemile Valley. The valley contains quite a few people and even more cattle. It's not a very appropriate place for wolves, but (for reasons nobody understands) wolves keep going there.

If he heads south and west of his present location, the black wolf will find his way to the Selway-Bitterroot, a large area of excellent wolf habitat in northern Idaho. The area offers plenty of food and as much unused wolf habitat as any region in the West. Other wolves that have come this way recently have not fared well, but perhaps this one would have better luck.

And if this young wolf were to keep trotting south for several days before hooking east a short distance, he would arrive at Yellowstone Park, the magic land of burping mud and faithful geysers. That wouldn't be far to go, not for a wolf. He would almost surely thrive if he discovered the park and its superabundance of bison, elk, and deer.

Perhaps he would then meet a female wolf and form a new wolf pack. If so, given the intense public interest in the return of wolves to Yellowstone, this young male would probably become the most famous wolf in the world. His photo would appear in magazines and newspapers. Someone would invent a name for him, and by that name he would be known to millions of people.

If the young wolf were to arrive at Yellowstone Park, he would become the most famous wolf in the world . . .

He might even make the cover of Time magazine.

He, of course, knows nothing about all this. He is just a wolf. All he knows is that he is hungry and lonely. He is a predator with a hollow belly, a pack animal without a pack.

A small cloud passes over the moon. The wolf flows along with the effortless, distance-eating gait of his kind. His long legs flash rhythmically, flicking mile after mile of landscape behind his plumed tail. He trots south, following ancient pathways used by wolves for centuries. His blocky feet make a putt-putt-putt noise in the crisp snow.

The wolves are returning.

They are coming home to lands where wolves lived since the glaciers left, but where none have been seen or heard for a long time—for years, for decades, for half a century, for several centuries.

Their return means different things to different people.

Late on an October night, Kathe Grooms is driving north on Highway 13, headed for our family cabin along the shores of Lake Superior. Molly, our teenaged daughter, sits beside Kathe and chatters about a movie she has just seen. She is trying to keep her mother alert. Deer are thick here, and our family has seen the messy results of several deer-auto collisions along this stretch of highway.

Near the mouth of the Brule River, the road bends sharply to the east.

Kathe's car takes that bend and is entering a gradual curve when two large animals appear in the headlights. They stop near the center of the highway and turn their majestic heads to study the approaching car.

"Deer, Molly! No. Are those . . . dogs?" Kathe knows there are no cabins nearby. It makes no sense that dogs would be out here at night.

For what seems like a long time, the animals do not move. In the Honda's headlights, their eyes glow with green fire like cyalume light sticks.

"WOLVES, Mom! They're WOLVES!"

Kathe is braking the car as rapidly as she dares.

The wolves are 30 feet from the car's bumper when they dive off the blacktop with athletic grace. They instantly disappear in the dense alder-aspen growth south of the road.

Molly has long adored wolves. Her room in our Minnesota home is virtually a shrine to wolves. Over the years, Molly has built up a serious library of wolf reference books, books her father would study while writing this book. Wolf researcher Dave Mech is a personal hero of Molly's. Blushing with awe, she met him once. Molly sleeps each night under the watchful gaze of 28 wolves in photos that hang on her walls.

Molly knows how special this moment is. Wisconsin only has a few dozen wild timber wolves, and she has just seen two of them. The car glides on through the night. Tears of joy well up in Molly's eyes.

Some of the wolves now repopulating former wolf country wear collars that beep locational signals to biologists. A few of those collars are state-of-the-art marvels that contain tiny electronic chips. Researchers with portable computers can call out to the chips, asking what the wolf has been doing lately. Some wolves that are recolonizing empty habitat wear collars that speak to satellites orbiting above earth's atmosphere.

Other wolves that are now returning to old wolf haunts wear only the classic badges of the hazardous life of a wolf—scars, torn ears, and various bones that fused together after they were snapped in fights with prey animals.

Two young women are backpacking in the Great Smoky Mountains National Park, in eastern Tennessee. One is studying a map when the other glimpses a dog-like animal darting through a sunlit clearing between two spruce stands.

She has just seen one of the rarest animals in the world: a free-living red wolf, one of the least understood and most

---

Wolves are returning home to lands where none have been seen for centuries.

endangered mammals in North America. This particular wolf is a key element in one of the most complex and frustrating programs in the history of wildlife management.

"That's so gross!" the hiker says. "Somebody's DOG is running around here. People who turn dogs loose in parks should be shot."

"A dog? That's strange. Maybe it was a coyote."

"Well, it looked like a coyote, actually. But it was a dog, alright. It was wearing a collar."

In some places, wolves are being restored to their former habitat with enormous effort and at considerable public expense. Many dedicated people—professionals and volunteers — work zealously to bring wolves back to places where they flourished before they were driven to the brink of extinction. If these people succeed, the wolves released into the wild will arrive as confused travelers in nylon dog kennels and will be freed in gradual steps, their progress followed closely by managers.

In other places, wolves are restocking themselves, coming in on their own. Nobody invited them. Nobody is helping them. They're simply doing what wolves have always done: striking out for new places to hunt, howl, mate, raise a family, and raise a new pack of wolves.

With or without human help, wolves are finding new places to hunt, howl, and raise a family.

Near Missoula, Montana, a woman hears a frenzied chorus of barking from the dogs behind her home. When she goes to her window, she spots a wolf sauntering up the draw behind her house.

She walks to the door and speaks to the animal.

"I see you," she says.

The wolf slides behind a tree in the orchard and stands there. It seems curious.

"You're not hiding," says the woman with a smile. "I can see you."

From behind the apple tree, the wolf studies the woman with its penetrating eyes.

A Mexican wolf paces restlessly in its zoo enclosure. This wolf's "habitat" is an artful duplication of the rocky, timbered country wolves occupied in the Southwest before federal agents and ranchers exterminated them.

Many of the lobos in zoos have little contact with their human keepers, and what contact they have is not pleasant. These wolves are not supposed to like people. They cannot be allowed to link people with food or companionship, for these wolves have a special destiny. If all goes well, they will be released into the wild.

But no matter how well that experiment goes, many of these extremely endangered wolves will die. Wild wolves have always died, of course, but the odds against these zoo-reared wolves will be formidable. They will be turned free with virtually no knowledge of how to live as a wild wolf. They will have none of the intimate knowledge of their surroundings that wild wolves depend upon. They won't know how to hunt for deer or how to kill one if they find it. They won't know how dangerous all vehicles and some people can be. Inevitably, many will die.

But the managers are determined to try.

Wolf restoration takes many forms.

A team of federal biologists and managers spends months preparing a wolf management plan outlining the proposed restoration of wolves to a particular region. The report is optimistic. The team sends its report to a supervisor, who passes it along to his supervisor.

Eventually the report is bucked up to the level of a political appointee in Washington. He doesn't know much about wildlife management, but he knows the politics of the issue. He calls a staff meeting, then issues a press release that basically says wolf restoration should be delayed until further study can resolve doubts.

A day later, in another Washington office not many blocks away, lawyers

---

"The wolf studies the woman with its penetrating eyes. . ."

and staff members for a national environmental group discuss this latest delay of the day that wolves will again run free in the West. They begin to prepare a lawsuit based on sections of the Endangered Species Act that give the U.S. Fish and Wildlife Service a mandate to restore endangered species.

The wheels of the legal process wrench into motion. Public meetings are held. When they turn out too favorably for wolf restoration, ranchers force federal managers to call more meetings in towns where they expect strong opposition to wolves. Congressional aides make phone calls back and forth. Wolf fans organize mailings. Agricultural lobbyists contact key politicians. Schoolchildren draw pictures of wolves smiling like dogs, which they mail to their representatives in Congress. A lean rancher squints into the camera of a rural television station and says, "I don't see how a buncha Eastern environmentalists can ram something like this down our throats. Won't be THEIR kids gettin' eaten by wolves!" He is sincerely scared.

Months later, in the air-conditioned loneliness of her chambers, a judge who has never seen a wolf pores over reams of biological and legal documents. The documents do not agree to any greater degree than the lawyers who filed them. Nothing in her law school background prepared the judge to make sense of all this. Nevertheless, she must soon render a decision that will advance, block, or delay wolf restoration.

This is how we make wildlife policy. We pretend the process is a contest of "law," a matter of making governmental policy conform to existing statutes. But it is not. It is a political struggle, pure and simple, more like mud wrestling than any high-minded pursuit. It has little to do with legal niceties and everything to do with power.

This, too, is part of the return of the wolves.

And all this time, wolves continue to come home, home to habitat where wolves flourished before being shot, trapped, snared, and poisoned. Many of them move at night, filtering through the underbrush unobserved.

It is a difficult comeback. Some of the returning wolves are illegally poisoned. Some are shot by people who mistake them for coyotes. Some are crushed under the wheels of speeding pickups. Some breed successfully, but then watch their pups sicken and slowly die of strange diseases against which evolution has given them no defenses.

But others survive. And every year, there are a few more of them. And then a few more.

It happens slowly, in many strange ways:

A man running a pulpwood stacking machine in Michigan's Upper Peninsula gets a prickly feeling down the back of his neck. He turns and finds he is being observed by a bemused gallery of half-grown wolf pups. The little wolves sit like sidewalk superintendents at a construction project. They obviously appreciate the show he is putting on for them. The next day, they are back again. And the next.

A survey in Yellowstone Park shows that an overwhelming percentage of visitors want to see wolves in the park. A survey in Idaho shows a large share of its citizens agree, as do most citizens of Wyoming and Montana. Public meetings about wolf restoration in the northern Rockies show that 60 to over 90 percent of the attendees support wolves. A Yale professor who has conducted many surveys evaluating the public's perception of wolves is moved to use language of a sort generally avoided by social scientists. He believes there is "a certain inexorable force" that makes wolf reintroduction "inevitable."

On a clear, windless night, excited eco-tourists travel a rough logging road in North Carolina's Alligator River National Wildlife Refuge. Their vehicles stop near a known red wolf den site. Giggling self-consciously, they prepare to howl to the wolves. One woman objects:

"I cain't do this! I've got this thick Georgia accent!" The biologist leading the group grins and reassures her: "Y'all go ahead. These are Dixie wolves!" Instinctively, the people howl as wolves do, with their round mouths tipped high to the sky.

A "big coyote" shot by a hunter in southeastern North Dakota turns out to be a wolf, probably from Minnesota. Months later, kitty-corner across the state, a rancher shoots another "big coyote" that turns out to be a wolf, probably from Canada. North Dakota managers realize they need to prepare management plans for an animal that hasn't been a significant part of the state's fauna in this century.

Two retired biologists in Idaho are stalking a pair of sandhill cranes feeding in a meadow, hoping to videotape the big birds. They're startled to notice that other animals are stalking the same cranes. In the next few minutes, the biologists film one of the rarest sights conceivable: two wolves hunting sandhill cranes in Idaho, a state where wolves have not lived continuously for many decades.

For some people, the return of wolves brings humans a precious gift. It is the gift of a second chance. These people urgently want to believe that our society is now a little

For some people, the return of the wolves gives humans the gift of a second chance.

wiser and kinder than our long, ugly history of wolf hatred would indicate.

These people realize they risk disappointment by banking so many hopes on the return of the wolf. They know that things won't be perfect when the wolves come back. Somewhere, a wolf is going to charge through a bawling mass of sheep like a chain saw. Somewhere, an embittered man is going to shoot a wolf, attach its beeper collar to a log, and throw it in a fast-flowing river just to spite biologists. These things happen, even now.

Nevertheless, the return of the wolf seems a momentous turning point in history. Wolves are returning, and their return offers humans a chance to demonstrate new tolerance and sensitivity in dealing with North America's most fascinating and controversial predator.

Surely, things cannot go as badly as they did the first time around.

A young couple living in the wilderness of northeastern Minnesota is roused from bed one sub-zero winter night by an insistent knocking on the cabin window. Who could possibly be calling on them at this hour?

The knocker turns out to be a wolf with a radio collar and badly diseased lungs. After some initial alarm and confusion, the two people carry the wolf into their cabin and place him by the warmth of the wood stove. He does not struggle.

Throughout the night, the wolf accepts their care as if this kindness is what he expected, what he came for. But compassion and warmth are not enough to heal his lungs. In the profound darkness of predawn, his breathing grows labored until, just at sunrise, he dies in their arms.

CHAPTER 2

Wolves and Humans

The wolf was once a great ecological success story. Wolves hunted all across Eurasia and the New World, from the latitude of sun-baked Mexico to the frozen Arctic. Wolves lived almost everywhere in the northern hemisphere except the most arid deserts and the highest mountains. And wherever they lived, wolves were the top predator of large mammals.

Today, wolves have been eliminated from almost all of their original range. In some places where they hang on, wolves occur in isolated remnant groups that seem doomed to fail. Wolves have not been heard for centuries in many places where they once thrived. Perhaps no species has fallen so low in so many places after succeeding in a diverse range of habitats.

The widespread collapse of wolf populations is all the more surprising when one considers the wolf's remarkable physical abilities and social structure. Most endangered species became endangered because they were too narrowly adapted, or because they could not respond to change. The wolf could not be more different. No hothouse flower, the wolf is one of the toughest, smartest, and most flexible species on earth. It should have been one of evolution's great winners, not a species struggling to avoid extinction in so many regions.

There is no dispute about how such an improbable collapse happened. Wolves have declined through no weakness of their own, but because they have been subjected to centuries of ferocious persecution by humans. With the possible exception of the coyote, no other North American species has been singled out for such systematic extermination. Particularly in the late 19th century, a concerted effort was made to eradicate wolves, as if they were a scourge that could not be tolerated at any level. That effort missed total success by the narrowest of margins.

Wolves once hunted all across the New World, from Mexico to the frozen Arctic.

Of course, humans have persecuted other animal species. Humans drove the bison to the brink of extinction, and people have traditionally killed venomous snakes on sight. Yet there is something uniquely ugly about the way humans have dealt with wolves. The wolf holds the wretched distinction of being the most misunderstood and persecuted animal in Western civilization. People have called wolves murderous, treacherous, gluttonous, and cowardly. As if that weren't enough, wolves have been damned from church pulpits as sulphur-breathing minions of the powers of chaos and evil. Humans have hated wolves for centuries with a curious hysterical energy.

Why?

WHO'S AFRAID OF THE BIG BAD WOLF?

It has become fashionable to blame wolf hatred on a few European fairy tales. After all, it was a wolf that threatened to flatten the homes of three little pigs. It was a wolf that swallowed the silly duck in "Peter and the Wolf." And above all, it was a wolf that gobbled Granny and seduced Little Red Riding Hood in a myth thought to represent male sexual aggression threatening feminine innocence. Some historians believe that this last story alone caused the deaths of millions of wolves.

But blaming old fairy tales doesn't explain much about our history of wolf hatred. It begs the question of

why wolves and not other predators were singled out as symbols of evil. And it grants too much influence to a handful of fables. The true origins of wolf hatred lie elsewhere.

Obviously, wolves have suffered because people feared them. Very few northern hemisphere animals are capable of killing humans. While biologists repeatedly tell us that wolves pose no threat to people, that's an extremely modern notion. Until the last years of the 20th century, even sophisticated people had no doubt that wolves attacked humans.

American settlers were probably less frightened by fairy tales than by all the apparently authentic stories about wolves attacking people. For some reason, Russia and France exported more than their share of these tales. A typical example is the Robert Browning poem "Ivan Ivanovitch," in which a wolf pack pursues a sleigh across a wintry Russian landscape. To save their own lives, the occupants throw children to the wolves.

A gory variant of that story was widely spread by newspapers just before World War I. This story described how "hundreds" of wolves devoured 118 out of a 120-member Russian wedding party. In a cowardly twist on the "women and children first" maxim, men from the wedding party pitched ladies and youngsters out of the sleighs. While the story seems comically macabre today, it was not questioned by readers in 1911.

Some bloody wolf stories had a basis in fact. The "Beasts of Gévaudan" were two animals that actually haunted a mountainous region of south-central France in the 1760s. The Beasts reportedly killed between 64 and 100 people before they were themselves destroyed. Because the Gévaudan animals were oddly colored and larger than normal wolves, modern researchers believe they were wolf-dog hybrids. But such subtle distinctions were lost on earlier people.

Wolves simply look scary. Predators tend to have elongated snouts, prominent teeth, and closely spaced eyes. Researchers have learned that a mask or puppet with similar features will frighten infants who have had no experience with predators. The stuffed toy animals we give infants differ as much as possible from that basic carnivorous predator profile. Consider the classic teddy bear, which distorts bear anatomy to produce a flat-nosed, wide-eyed toy that infants find reassuring.

Admirers of wolves today can't understand how people ever failed to

appreciate the beauty of wolves. One answer lies in the way wolves were rendered by artists in earlier times. If an artist exaggerates certain features—the snout becomes longer and thinner, the teeth more prominent, the eyes narrower—a lovely animal appears menacing. If the wolf is also depicted as gaunt and desperately hungry, it becomes all the more threatening. By taking small liberties, an artist can make a handsome animal appear ghastly.

By contrast, contemporary Americans visualize wolves as they appear in photographs and paintings. The models for the newer works are captive wolves that, while not quite chubby, are fed well and look healthy. The wolves we see in photos appear noble, friendly, and intelligent. They seem more like loving pets than slavering demons of the night.

Early Europeans and American settlers were also apparently unnerved by the fact that wolves run in packs. Old wolf stories routinely featured packs much larger than any groups researchers have discovered. The story of "hundreds" of wolves gobbling the wedding party is just one example. The exaggeration betrays the uneasiness people felt toward a predator that could surround and overwhelm its prey with superior numbers. If one thinks that one might end up as the prey, the idea of being encircled by wolves is disquieting.

All in all, it's too easy for contemporary Americans to belittle the fears of earlier people. The settlers living on the ragged fringes of civilization spent sleepless nights while wolves keened and moaned from the forests nearby. Those people not only "knew" that wolves killed humans but assumed that the animals would seize any chance to do so. They feared wolves in ways that are impossible for us to appreciate today.

THE HOUND FROM HELL

The Christian religion has been another source of wolf hatred.

The few references to wolves in the Bible are anything but flattering. The central Biblical metaphor presents Jesus as the shepherd whose flock consists of his true believers. The image of Christians as sheep is not particularly flattering, especially to anyone who understands sheep, but the real loser in this metaphor is the wolf. If Christians are sheep, wolves (since they prey on sheep) are murderers at best and possibly agents of the devil.

Wolves acquired all sorts of demonic significance in the tortured

imaginations of medieval Europeans. Priests began preaching that wolves were Satan's minions. A 15th-century council of theologians studied the best research on the topic and proclaimed that werewolves undoubtedly existed. As a consequence, several men were burned at the stake or buried alive after confessing to murders they committed while they believed they were werewolves. A young man named Jean Grenier made a similar confession, but his death sentence was commuted. Grenier spent the last years of his life in a friary, running around on all fours, eating rotten meat, and believing himself to be a wolf. It was so common for demented people to believe they were wolves that a name, lycanthropy, was coined to identify the malady.

Wolves somehow became associated with all the carnal appetites the church wanted to discipline and suppress. Incongruously, wolves—who are lucky indeed if they experience sex once a year—were depicted as

Some historians believe that the story of Little Red Riding Hood (illustrated above) caused the deaths of millions of wolves.

symbols of promiscuity by the species with the most hedonistic sex life in the animal kingdom!

THE BEAST OF WASTE AND DESOLATION

When European settlers began to carve small enclaves of civilization into the wilderness of North America, wolves became symbols of chaos and economic waste. Puritan preachers exhorted their flocks to make a "fruitful field" out of the "howling wilderness." The howl of the wilderness was supplied, of course, by the wolf. Wolves were associated with all the godless wastelands that were not yet tamed and made safe for civil life and economic productivity.

The people who settled North America believed that mankind should hold dominion over animals. Animals were seen as valuable to the extent that they served man's needs (an idea with strong adherents today). From such a utilitarian perspective, wolves are worse than useless. They not only lack intrinsic economic value, they destroy valuable livestock and wildlife.

Both wolves and Native Americans were reviled as impediments to Manifest Destiny, the inevitable expansion of civilization from the Atlantic to the Pacific. Even those early Americans who admired Indians

Large ungulates, like the fallen mule deer shown above, are the wolf's natural prey.

and wolves assumed they had to be eliminated because nothing could stand in the way of the westward march of progress.

When much of the West was sectioned off into large livestock ranches, wolf hatred reached heights that seem barbaric even in the context of an already-bloody relationship. Cattlemen laced carrion with ground glass and left it for the wolves. Trapped wolves were released with their jaws wired shut, so they would die slowly. Wolves were set ablaze, much as "werewolves" had been burned at the stake in the middle ages.

Livestock interests kept pressing for more anti-predator programs to make the West safe for cattle and sheep. All levels of government supported the effort to eradicate wolves. Though these programs were called "wolf control," there was nothing controlled—nothing measured— about them.

One of the most enthusiastic federal wolf control agents in the 1930s was a young biologist named Aldo Leopold. Leopold believed that eliminating wolves would not only protect livestock but restore depleted stocks of elk, deer, and other game animals in the West.

The growing popularity of sport hunting provided another rationale for destroying wolves. Hunters believed that every deer, moose, or elk killed by wolves was one less game animal available for humans. Killing wolves was an appealing form of game management, because it promised to create abundant game populations without requiring humans to restrain their harvest of the game animals.

TWO PREDATORS AT THE TOP OF THE FOOD CHAIN

People who try to explain wolf hatred are drawn to intellectual analyses of history. The elegance of those explanations makes them attractive, yet they might distract us from a more basic and primitive motivation for wolf hatred—namely competition. Humans have hated wolves because wolves compete with us for food.

We know that large ungulates, from bighorn sheep to moose, are the wolves' natural prey. Those same animals (if we can include domestic sheep and cattle) are the preferred food of humans. One might argue that the conflict is not necessary. Wolves have no choice. They are programmed by physiology and social organization to consume large ungulates and cannot switch to other foods. Humans prize such wild game as elk and deer for complicated social and historical reasons. People prefer to eat beef, veal, and lamb for various economical and gastronomical reasons. But there is no point in debating taste. At some level, whenever wolves consume a cow or moose, humans are apt to think, "Hey! That's one less for us!"

This natural competition has resulted in a pattern seen in almost every area where wolves and humans coexist. First humans wipe out or deplete the wolves' natural food. Then they refill the empty habitat with domestic livestock. When wolves turn to the only remaining food source—domestic animals—people respond with deadly force.

Wolves and humans are both predators sitting at the top of the food chain. Actually, what we call the "food chain" is more of a food pyramid, with a broad base of vegetation, a smaller midsection composed of prey animals, and a very narrow peak composed of predators. It is one of the most basic and inescapable axioms of biology that food pyramids cannot support very many predators. One of the corollaries of that principle seems to be that predators don't happily share a prey base, which is the usual explanation offered for the intolerance that wolves display toward coyotes and dogs.

WOLF HATRED AS SELF-HATRED

Even after contemplating the many factors causing humans to fear and resent wolves, it's difficult to account for the virulence of wolf hatred. Ultimately, it seems that wolves have suffered because they remind us too much of ourselves. This theme has been worked out in convincing detail by the writer Barry Lopez.

Through the centuries, Lopez argues, we have projected onto the wolf the qualities we most despise and fear in ourselves. Wolves have not simply been misperceived, but demonized and scapegoated in a paroxysm of self-contempt. Repeatedly, the wolf we have persecuted is not the *actual* wolf that hunts and howls in lonely places, but a conceived wolf we have invented somewhere in the spooky nether regions of our own psyches.

THE NEW POSSIBILITY

Two or three decades ago, the story of men and wolves would have ended on that tragic note. But something has happened recently to alter the old relationship, something dramatically new and almost as difficult to understand as wolf hatred.

No person influenced American attitudes toward wildlife more

Two or three decades ago, it seemed that the story of wolves and humans would end on a tragic note.

fundamentally than Aldo Leopold, so it's fitting that an incident in Leopold's life marks the start of a new perception of wolves. Leopold and some companions were riding in the White Mountains of New Mexico when they saw a female wolf swim a river. She was met by six large pups that wriggled joyously to celebrate her return. The men's response was as reflexive as swatting a mosquito: They began blazing away with rifles. Then they examined the results of their shooting. A wounded pup dragged itself into the rocks, while its mother lay bleeding by the riverbank.

Something astonishing happened. Looking into the eyes of the dying she-wolf, Leopold's sense of triumph changed to remorse:

We reached the old wolf in time to watch a fierce green fire dying in her eyes. I realized then, and have known ever since, that there was something new to me in those eyes—something known only to her and to the mountain. I was young then, and full of trigger-itch; I thought that because fewer wolves meant more deer, that no wolves would mean hunters' paradise. But after seeing the green fire die, I sensed that neither the wolf nor the mountain would agree with such a view.

In that remarkable moment, centuries of wolf hatred collided with the basic decency and growing ecological wisdom of a single man . . . and the great shift from wolf hatred to wolf admiration became possible. It wouldn't happen soon—not even for Leopold, who continued to advocate wolf control for some time—but a new understanding of wolves was now possible.

Adolph Murie established himself as the pioneer of modern wolf research when he undertook his classic study of wolves in Alaska's Mount McKinley Park during the early 1940s. Murie had the discipline and honesty to see wolves as they were, not as he had been told they were. He described wolves as affectionate, cooperative animals that live in ecological balance with game populations. But few people were paying attention, and the killing went on.

A new climate of ecological awareness was being born three decades later when researcher L. David Mech brought out his book, *The Wolf*, in 1970. Mech wrote at a time when bounties had just been removed from wolves in Minnesota. The general public mostly ignored wolves, while many hunters and farmers hated them. Although *The Wolf* seems primarily addressed to scholars and students of wolves, the book became a crossover hit that sold well to the increasing legions of wolf fans. Mech, an energetic and multi-talented man, continues to pursue his favorite topic as a researcher, writer, manager, and photographer. More than any single person, he is responsible for creating a sophisticated, accurate, and tolerant public perception of wolves.

Shortly after Mech's book appeared, the U.S. Congress passed the Endangered Species Act of 1973. Wolves were among the first animals listed as endangered. That status brought wolves into the public eye and endowed them with a certain tragic, romantic identity they had never before enjoyed. Federal policy

took a remarkable about-face. Managers began plotting the restoration of wolves in regions where governmental programs had only recently succeeded in eliminating them.

It's impossible to document the impact of the countless wolf films that have aired on television in recent years. Beyond question, they have been potent agents for changing the public perception of wolves. Before Murie, virtually no human had actually seen wolves without intervening veils of fear and myth. Now, that experience is routinely available to anyone with a television.

In just a decade and a half, the wolf has gone from scapegoat to object of adoration. Wolves have become the

Today, wolves have become the ultimate symbol of wilderness.

ultimate symbols of wilderness and of man's inhumanity to animals. Artists who once made a living cranking out waterfowl paintings now frequent zoo wolf exhibits to gain familiarity with the animal that now dominates the wildlife art market. The Minnesota town of Ely, notorious in the 1970s as a bastion of wolf hatred, scrapped vigorously in the 1980s for the privilege of hosting the International Wolf Center. Mail-order catalogs can sell any product imaginable so long as it carries the image of a wolf. Americans are falling in love with wolves.

Library bookshelves now groan under the weight of all the revis-ionist, pro-wolf juvenile fiction. In *The True Story of the Three Little Pigs,* the author ("A. Wolf") protests, "Hey, I was framed!"

While children are still aware of the Little Red Riding Hood legend, they're more likely to identify with *Julie of the Wolves.* In that highly popular book, a little girl rejected by humans is befriended by wolves. Many youngsters who read now have a positive image of wolves.

Such a large change . . . and in just a decade or two! How could this have happened? According to one juvenile literature librarian, today's children are pro-wolf because books now

There are now three wolves keeping company with one another in the American mind.

"present the scientific perspective on wolves." Really?

Are we witnessing the triumph of science over ignorance?

Consider Farley Mowat's *Never Cry Wolf*. Originally a book, it became a hit movie that lives on in television re-runs and video rentals. By presenting wolves as admirable and humans as vicious, *Never Cry Wolf* did for wolves what the movie *Dances With Wolves* later did for Indians: turned a long-lived stereotype on its head.

Never Cry Wolf must have presented unusual conflicts for wolf biologists like Mech. The book was a work of fiction that the author presented as nonfiction. In the act of rejecting pernicious old myths, Mowat created pernicious new ones. For example, wolves cannot live on a diet of mice, no matter what wolf admirers might prefer to believe. Some scientists were disturbed because they believed Mowat plagiarized some of his material. Yet in spite of its flaws and distortions, *Never Cry Wolf* was attractively written and sympathetic to wolves at a time when wolves badly needed friends.

Can a bad book be a good thing?

THE THREE WOLVES

The strange, anguished relationship between humans and wolves has thus taken another odd turn.

There are now three different wolves keeping uneasy company with one another in the North American mind. The old demonic wolf lives on, especially in the minds of older, rural Americans. Their view is being refuted by rapidly growing numbers of wolf fans, many of whom adore wolves uncritically and regard them as nobler than most humans. Then there is the wolf of the biologist: a remarkable predator—neither demon nor saint—that has an odd ability to incite contentious management controversies. Unfortunately, the sober, factual image of the wolf is harder to promote than the other two.

Wolves were persecuted for centuries because they were reduced to symbols of evil. Now they are venerated by people who reduce them to symbols of wilderness (once a negative value, now positive) and embodiments of man's many crimes against the natural world. People used to view wolves imperfectly through filters of fear; they now view them imperfectly through filters of guilt and romance.

After all this time, it remains almost as difficult as ever to see wolves—not as symbols, but as wolves.

CHAPTER 3

Wolves of North America

All carnivores evolved from an ancient group of meat-eaters called creodonts. Creodonts were otter-like creatures that may have slept in trees. They gave rise to two new types of carnivores. One was a cat-like group that lived mostly in forests and jungles, practicing an ambush style of predation. The other was a dog-like group that moved onto the plains and evolved long, speedy limbs to run down prey.

In time, that second group produced the highly successful family of Canidae, the dog-like animals. It consists of several genera, the most prominent being the genus *Canis*. Included in the genus are the gray wolf, *Canis lupus*, the red wolf, Canis rufus, the domestic dog, *Canis familiaris*, the coyote, *Canis latrans*, several jackals, and Ruppell's fox.

THE WOLVES OF PREHISTORY

Scientists have reconstructed the history of wolf evolution primarily through the painstaking process of analyzing fossil evidence. Conclusions gained in the course of such research are now being corrected through sophisticated analyses of genetic material. Those two sources of information recently allowed prominent wolf taxonomist Ron Nowak to propose a fascinating account of how today's wolves developed over time.

According to Nowak, coyotes evolved from foxes some four or five million years ago. Between one and two million years ago, the coyote line split into two groups. One group consisted of a slightly huskier version of today's coyote. The other group had more massive skulls and other wolf-like features. This new group, in fact, closely resembled today's red wolf.

These wolfish coyotes underwent many changes in the Pleistocene, which is probably the most turbulent and intriguing evolutionary epoch. In the Pleistocene, the only constant factor was change. Ice caps formed, melted, and formed again. Seas rose

Wolves may have evolved from coyotes between one and two million years ago.

and fell. Islands appeared and disappeared. From time to time, glaciers surged southward to reshape the land like runaway bulldozers—scalping off hills, throwing up new ones, and generally altering the face of the earth. Most significantly, the Bering land bridge appeared and disappeared, alternately connecting and isolating the American and Eurasian continents from each other.

Changing climates produced changing forage, which in turn fostered changes in the fauna. Glaciation and other events isolated animal populations for long enough periods to let them evolve uniquely.

Then the reversal of those conditions set them free to move about again. In short, the Pleistocene was a sort of laboratory in which evolution could run riot, experimenting with all possibilities and producing all manner of beasts.

And what beasts! They included giant condors, saber-toothed tigers, wild pigs big enough to bare teeth three feet long, and the aurochs, a highly belligerent bison that managed to survive into the 17th century. The Pleistocene also saw multiple tests of the "bigger is better" concept. This was a time of monster elk whose freakishly large antlers reached up to

The two skulls illustrate that a wolf is significantly larger than a coyote.

ten feet above the ground. In the Pleistocene, beavers were as big as today's brown bears, and bears were twice the size of today's grizzly. Towering over them all was the imperial mammoth, a sort of elephant that was as large as many of the great dinosaurs.

Wolves underwent many changes in this seething, complex time. The original wolves, smallish animals that hardly differed from coyotes, slipped across the Bering land bridge to invade Eurasia. They eventually landed in such places as Spain, Japan, and several countries of the Middle East. Some of those regions still contain populations of small, "primitive" wolves.

Meanwhile, in northern Eurasia, a cooling climate favored the development of a larger and more formidable wolf. This larger wolf eventually got the chance to return to the American continent. There it met at least two other wolves, the original coyote-like red wolf and an impressive animal called the "dire wolf." Dire wolves had massive skulls and prodigious teeth. Most dire wolves were significantly larger than today's wolves. Dire wolves apparently evolved their unique qualities in South America, later migrating back to North America.

The various types of wolf coexisted for some time, and skulls of gray and dire wolves have been found together in California's La Brea tar pits. The dire wolf eventually disappeared, either because it didn't fare well in a time when prey animals were not so large, or because early humans eliminated a predator that competed directly with them for favored prey.

Wolves underwent their most recent evolution in central Alaska, in a time when the region was a green refuge surrounded by glaciers. Conditions favored the development of a larger gray wolf. Those wolves eventually spread out, invading western Canada, the Rocky Mountain area, and much of Siberia.

Thus the large gray wolves that developed in central Alaska are the most "modern" or recently evolved. Most wolf populations located far from Alaska represent smaller and earlier versions of the gray wolf. The oldest and most primitive of all wolves is the red wolf of the southeastern U.S., an animal virtually identical to the very first wolf of all.

WOLVES AND DOGS

"Man's best friend," the domestic dog, is basically a wolf modified by selective breeding. Ponder that for a moment. A clipped and coiffed miniature poodle in a snug knitted jacket is—believe it or not—a cousin of the wolf. So similar are dogs and wolves, in fact, that some scientists consider them variants of one species.

Wolves and dogs are identical in several biological respects. For example, the gestation period for both is 63 days. The most sophisticated genetic sampling techniques to date have failed, in spite of much effort, to find any genetic markers that differentiate dogs from wolves. Many dog habits that perplex their owners (such as urinating on fire hydrants or howling at police sirens) are understandable to anyone who recognizes the wolf behaviors from which they derive.

Genetic similarity does not equate with social compatibility. Wolves, dogs, and coyotes are likely to kill each other if circumstances allow. That probably results from a basic, instinctive sense of competition. The more similar species are in size and form, the more directly they compete for the same food supply. The hypothetical poodle mentioned above might wear a collar embellished with a series of shiny metal brads. Those little brads are merely a fashion statement today, but they derive from the sharp spikes once attached to dog collars as protection against wolf attacks.

The different canids share more genetic compatibility than is common between different species. As one consequence, canids can and do interbreed to produce fertile offspring. Of course, social barriers usually prevent hybridization. But wolf-dog, wolf-coyote, and coyote-dog crosses occasionally occur in the wild. And some people continue to breed wolf-dog hybrids, despite the fact that many authorities condemn the practice as irresponsible.

Canid interbreeding sometimes frustrates the biologists and managers working to restore wolf populations. The most tragic example was the hybridization between coyotes and red wolves that almost destroyed the red wolf as a species. Managers trying to restore gray wolves typically keep careful records of wolf sightings as one index of how well the wolves are doing. But some "wolf" sightings turn out to be wolf-dog hybrids someone has released in the wild. For example, managers in the state of Washington were frustrated to find that a "wolf" they had trapped and fitted with a radio collar was in fact a wolf-dog hybrid. Because they're not as wary as true wolves, wolf-dog hybrids sometimes attack livestock or even people. That complicates life for wolf managers, as the aggression of hybrids often diminishes public tolerance of wolves.

Wolves and dogs are identical in several biological respects.

WOLVES AND THEIR PREY

Wolves evolved to prey upon ungulates, a term referring to all the large, hoofed mammals. Prominent ungulates include deer, elk, moose, sheep, and bison. Those animals are large, quick, and difficult to hunt. Most are hard to catch, and some, especially moose, are dangerous when attacked. Wolves could never prey efficiently on ungulates had they not learned to hunt cooperatively in groups.

This innovation—hunting in packs—is probably the most significant and unusual aspect of the wolf as a predator. Solitary predators are usually obliged to prey on animals their own size or smaller. But by hunting in cooperative groups, a pack of smaller predators can successfully take a large prey animal. When wolves attack a moose, each wolf is giving away a *ten-to-one weight advantage*. To understand the magnitude of that feat, consider the African lion, which weighs nine times as much as a wolf, yet rarely pursues prey as large as a moose. The pack style of hunting is obviously a major reason that wolves were so successful before falling victim to human persecution. Early human societies developed a very similar hunting style.

Large ungulates (deer-sized or larger) are the natural prey of wolves. Since few other predators can take large ungulates, it could be said that

When wolves attack a moose, each wolf is attacking an animal ten times its own size.

wolves evolved their pack hunting style in order to take advantage of an abundant food source that was not being exploited. It might also be said that wolves preyed on large ungulates because no other prey animals were large and abundant enough to reward the hunting efforts of a whole pack. This is a chicken-and-egg debate that chases its own tail; the point is that large ungulates are the logical prey for wolf packs.

Both wolves and their prey underwent millennia of evolutionary refinement in a process that biologists have likened to an arms race. When evolution produced a new and improved antelope—for example, a swifter model—only the quickest wolves could catch it. Because only the speediest wolves then lived long enough to reproduce, their genes brought about new and improved versions of wolves. The idea is neatly expressed in a Robinson Jeffers poem:

> *What but the wolf's tooth*
> *whittled so fine*
> *The fleet limbs of the antelope?*

THE TWO WOLVES

North America contains two basic wolves, the gray wolf and the red wolf.

The animal most Americans mean when they say "wolf" is the gray wolf.

Many people call these animals "timber wolves," but the eastern timber wolf is just one of several subtypes of gray wolf. The gray wolf was once widespread and common in North America. In fact, it originally occurred all over the northern hemisphere, from the latitude of Mexico City and north almost to the North Pole.

According to taxonomist E.A. Goldman, 24 subtypes of gray wolves once roamed North America. But Goldman proposed that highly fragmented breakdown at a time when taxonomic "splitters" were dominant. "Lumpers" have prevailed recently, arguing that the similarities among gray wolf subtypes are far more important than the differences (which often derive from minor variations in appearance). The gray wolf that today chases deer in Minnesota is essentially identical to the extinct "buffalo wolf" of the Great Plains; just as the wolf that once hunted stags in Scotland was essentially identical to the wolves that still live in Siberia.

The red wolf, *Canis rufus*, is a special case. If it is a wolf, it is a distinct species rather than a subtype of the gray wolf. Taxonomists continue to debate the legitimacy of the red wolf's standing as a species. Some believe it is actually a wolf-coyote hybrid, for

---

The animal most Americans mean when they say "wolf" is the gray wolf.

the red wolf falls between the gray wolf and the coyote in size, appearance, and some behavioral traits. But if modern taxonomists such as Nowak are right, the red wolf is not only a true wolf but has a special status as the original wolf, from which the gray wolf derived.

Biologists will probably never uncover enough reliable information about the original ranges of the two North American wolves, because wolves were often extirpated before scientists could make careful observations. However, that statement lets the scientists off too lightly. For far too long, biologists didn't consider wolves worth studying. Serious scholarship on wolves began only about half a century ago.

In broad terms, though, the story of the range of North America's wolves is simple enough.

The red wolf is believed to have originally occurred in certain regions of the American Southeast, from coastal Georgia and Florida as far west as Texas. It might have lived as far north as the Carolinas and southern Illinois.

The gray wolf was far more widespread. It originally lived almost

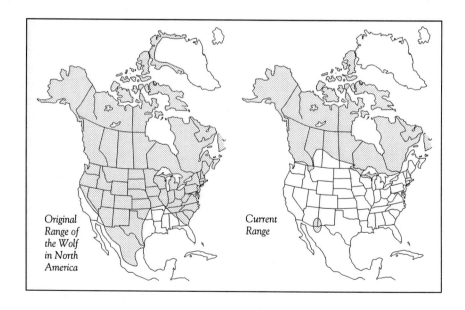

Original Range of the Wolf in North America

Current Range

everywhere on the North American continent, except for a patch of the Southeast that more or less corresponds to the range of the red wolf. Gray wolves occurred as far south as Mexico City, although not in the land adjacent to either coast of Mexico, or in the Baja or Pacific coasts of California.

FIVE ARENAS

The wolf is the most controversial animal in North America. Where wolves don't exist, people fight about plans to restore them; where they do exist, people fight over plans to manage them. Even if Americans learn to tolerate and respect wolves, the details of their management will always provoke political discussion.

That is why, in many ways, the most important distinction between different wolves today is not anatomical but political. For example, while several of Goldman's gray wolf subtypes live in Alaska, it makes more sense to talk about the management of wolves within a political boundary rather than management of a mix of subspecies.

In the political sense, then, there are five arenas for disputes about wolf

management in the United States.

Three management controversies relate to three subtypes of the gray wolf. In each case, the U.S. Fish and Wildlife Service has prepared a comprehensive "recovery plan" to serve as a blueprint for restoring wolves to some portion of their former range.

The oldest recovery plan deals with the eastern timber wolf of Minnesota, Wisconsin, and Michigan. This plan has been so successful it seems about to put itself out of existence. That is, wolves are likely to lose their official endangered status in the Upper Midwest.

Another recovery plan has been prepared for the northern Rocky Mountain wolf of Montana, Idaho, and Wyoming. Disputes about this program have centered on the battle to restore wolves to Yellowstone Park, although the plan deals with the entire region. The Yellowstone wolf controversy has developed into one of those unique watershed management disputes that have great symbolic and historic importance.

A third recovery plan has been developed for restoring the Mexican wolf or "lobo," a subtype of the gray wolf, to isolated bits of habitat in

Texas, New Mexico, and Arizona. Mexican wolves are in far more perilous condition than their northern cousins. The successful recovery of the lobo would represent one of the most remarkable victories in the history of wildlife management.

A separate recovery plan exists to restore the red wolf in limited areas of the American Southeast. This program, now several years old, has produced results that are extremely encouraging for the several gray wolf restoration programs. Techniques developed in the red wolf effort may go a long way toward shaping programs to restore wolves in the West and Southwest.

Alaska is an unusual case. No recovery plan exists for Alaska's wolves because they have not been extirpated or even diminished to "threatened" status. In fact, Alaska's wolves seem to be flourishing. Yet Alaska's wolf management has been extremely controversial. While this book is about the return of wolves, we will discuss Alaska (where wolves can't return because they've never gone away) because the state has more wolves than any other, and because its wolf management has been the subject of bitter disputes.

CHAPTER 4

Meet the Wolf

Gray wolves are sometimes gray, but they can also be rusty red, cream, tawny, or buff. The pure black color phase that humans find so unnerving often occurs in regions of Canada and Alaska. The wolves of some regions, including the high Arctic islands of Canada and Greenland, are creamy white. Pups from a single litter can have coats of different colors, and packs commonly include animals of different colors. If wolves discriminate against one another on the basis of color, the practice has escaped the eye of scientists.

Perhaps the most common pattern is a silver-gray body with light tan legs. Wolf coats typically show considerable variation in shading, as if the animal had been airbrushed by an artist in a hurry. The shading on a wolf's face, like a clown's makeup, dramatizes its changing expressions.

In effect, wolves wear two coats. The downy, highly insulating undercoat is so thick that a pointed finger can't penetrate through it to the skin beneath. When we look at a wolf, though, we mostly see the long, glossy guard hairs of the overcoat. Wolf fur has the unusual quality of not accumulating ice when struck with warm, moist breath. Consequently, in Alaska and other places that suffer from bitter winters, residents have been known to compromise their anti-trapping beliefs by rimming their parka hoods with a luxurious ruff of wolf fur.

The wolf's majestic head frames a pair of eyes that are variously described as yellow, amber, or green. Lois Crisler, who lived with several semi-tame wolves in Alaska, described wolf eyes as "level and large and as clear as pure water, gray or gold or green according to mood and individual wolf." Some Native Americans considered the eyes of the wolf the only other "human" thing in the world. When a wolf takes an interest in something, it studies the object with an intent but calm expression. People who find them-

selves the subject of a wolf's stare are often moved to awe by the sense of power and intelligence it conveys. The ancient Greeks believed the wolf's gaze could strike a person dumb.

Of all dog breeds, the malamute most closely resembles the wolf. Comparing a wolf to a malamute of the same size suggests interesting ways in which wolves differ from dogs. For starters, the wolf's brain is 30 percent larger. Scientists don't know if the extra capacity results in superior intelligence or greater sensory detection. Wolves have wider heads than dogs. That effect is accentuated by the "ruff"—those long, down-slanting hairs that flank the wolf's face and give it a striking profile. The wolf's snout is longer and thinner, probably because humans have bred dogs to look less threatening. A wolf's chest is narrower and deeper, and a wolf is much leggier than a dog of the same size. The lanky legs of the wolf terminate in feet twice as big as those of a comparably-sized dog. (A wolf paw is

The ancient Greeks believed a wolf's gaze could strike a person dumb.

the size of an average man's fist.) Wolves hold their tails many ways, but never in the characteristic manner of many dogs, curled up over the back. People who have spent time around wolves often find themselves contemptuous of the dog's tail posture, because it seems foppish and undignified compared to the tail postures assumed by wolves.

Wolves are adapted for living in cold climates. When a wolf wraps itself in a ball and tucks its nose in the insulating muff of its tail, it can sleep in minus 50-degree weather. A wolf's massive feet help it move on snow. Because of its narrow chest, the front legs are mounted close together. This arrangement enables wolves to run efficiently, laying down tracks in a single neat line. It is a useful adaptation for an animal that must often break a path through snow.

A wolf makes its living with a set of 42 teeth. The most impressive are the four large canine teeth. The big canines are one-and-a-quarter inches long. Their primary purpose is to pierce the hair and hide of such shaggy brutes as moose, so the wolf can gain a secure hold. The molars at the back of the jaw have the power to crunch huge moose, elk, and bison leg bones. Between the molars and canines are the carnassial teeth, which shear skin, sinew, and muscle. But wolves can also use their teeth for delicate tasks. Lois Crisler once woke from a nap with an odd sensation. One of her wolves was grooming her, gently tugging individual eyelashes with its massive canine teeth.

Wolves are smaller than most people think they are. Most gray wolves weigh between 50 and 100 pounds, with females running about 20 percent smaller than males. Size is related to geography. The wolves of some desert regions may not exceed 45 pounds, while weights of 115 pounds are not uncommon in cold regions. The largest wolves come from Alaska, the Yukon, some areas of Canada, and the former Soviet Union. Those regions occasionally produce individuals weighing 175 pounds. Wolf researcher Dave Mech mentions an unconfirmed report of a Yukon wolf weighing *227 pounds*. That animal would have created a stir if it had strolled through a 16th-century French village!

In length, male wolves approximate the height of most humans: They are from five to six-and-a-half feet long (nose to tail-tip). Of that length, about 18 inches is tail. Male wolves usually stand 26 to 32 inches at the shoulder, so an average man could stand with a leg on either side of a wolf at the shoulders. One old trapper from northwestern Wisconsin talked about a wolf so large it walked in snowdrifts three feet deep without creasing the snow with its chest. Well, maybe. Old trappers knew a lot about wolves, but some of them were reluctant to let facts interfere with a good story.

THE WOLF'S SENSES

Biologists don't know a great deal about the sensory capabilities of wolves. Serious wolf study began only a few decades ago, and there have been more urgent questions to answer than how well a wolf can see or hear.

While a blind wolf wouldn't live long, scientists consider vision the wolf's least developed sense. Vision primarily becomes important to wolves during hot chases when the prey is near. Wolves can apparently detect moving objects at distances where they cannot discern stationary objects. They see very well at night, and that's important. Especially in areas where they're heavily persecuted by humans, wolves do much of their traveling and hunting in the dark.

A wolf's sense of hearing is at least as acute as a human's and probably much more so. A wolf's concave external ear funnels sound vibrations to the inner ear much like a human cupping a hand behind an ear to detect faint sounds. Wolves can hear howls as far as six miles away, possibly ten miles away in open terrain. They can also discriminate between tones that are very similar. A genuine human howl is more likely to provoke a response than a tape-recorded wolf howl. This suggests that wolves detect something phony in a tape recording that sounds perfectly authentic to humans.

Biologists claim that wolves are a hundred times better at sensing odors than humans, and some say a *million* times better. Researchers have seen wolves scenting prey a mile and a half away, although that would necessarily involve a favorable wind. Wolves detect odors that humans cannot. They can identify many individual scents within the complex jumble of odors they encounter from moment to moment. Because humans cannot detect scents as wolves do, it seems likely that scent plays a much larger role in a wolf's life than scientists have yet documented.

A Michigan biologist once tracked two wolves along a snowmobile trail. After miles of straight trotting, one wolf dove 35 feet off the trail and jammed its muzzle into the snow. Why? When the biologist examined

the face-shaped hole in the snow, he found a tiny patch of wolf fur there. The traveling wolf smelled that snippet of fur buried beneath six inches of snow from a distance of 12 yards.

Wolves are highly intelligent. I'm not aware of any empirical studies measuring wolf intelligence, but there is abundant anecdotal evidence. A retired wolf trapper once claimed that wolves would occasionally hit one of his snares but escape by dodging back quickly. When that happened, said the trapper, he could forget about putting out any snare sets for that wolf . . . or any wolf in that pack.

After one wolf learned about snares, the entire pack would become wary of the traps.

Some captive wolves learn to escape from their pens, after which they are almost impossible to confine in any enclosure. These Houdinis do not escape through random effort, but by using remarkable problem-solving powers. Wolves have remembered former human masters after a separation of three years.

Wolves seem especially adept at learning by observation. Some learn to open doors with their mouths after watching people using doorknobs. A

Wolves can smell objects buried beneath deep snow.

research assistant once created a machine that would dispense a tasty morsel when its treadle was pressed. He taught the use of this machine to a wolf in an enclosure. When he later attempted to teach the machine to a second wolf, he was dumbfounded to discover that this wolf already understood the whole business. The second wolf had observed the earlier demonstration from its nearby enclosure.

Because wolves live in groups, all pack members can benefit from the experience of one wolf. The ability to learn by observation must have benefited wolves enormously over the centuries.

WOLF CAPABILITIES

The mobility of wolves is legendary. According to a Russian proverb, "The wolf is fed by his feet." On the tundra, where prey animals are separated by great distances, wolves may travel 40 miles a day to feed. A wolf usually trots along at five to nine miles an hour, maintaining that pace for hours. Pressed by hunters, one wolf pack in Finland moved 124 miles in a single day. Packs have traveled 45 miles in a day even without such provocation. Two wolves in British Columbia broke trail in five feet of snow for 22 miles. A wolf is generally on the move for

eight hours a day, so wolves spend a third of their lives (about half of their waking hours) trotting or running. It's unlikely that any human athlete, such as a world-class marathon runner, could match the aerobic conditioning of the average wolf.

When attacking, wolves can turn on a burst of speed of up to 35 miles an hour. They explode toward their prey in bounds that cover as much 16 feet each. Wolves can maintain a hot chase speed of 25 miles an hour for up to 20 minutes, although most chases are either abandoned or concluded with a kill much sooner than that.

Wolves exert a bite-pressure of 1,500 pounds per square inch—twice the crunch of a German shepherd. If that's difficult to visualize, a biologist once told me such pressure is equal to the pressure on the bottom of a broom stick that's weighted down by a Volkswagen Beetle. If *that's* difficult to picture, just remember that wolves can crush the massive thigh bones of moose and bison. Wolves caught in leg-hold traps sometimes vent their frustration on nearby trees. A researcher told me wolves can snap through saplings an inch-and-a-half thick "like they were cooked celery."

A wolf also possesses tremendous body strength. A friend once found the hind leg of a moose calf. One or

---

As the Russians say it, "The wolf is fed by his feet."

two wolves had dragged the rest of the body so far away that he never located the rest of the carcass. The hind leg alone weighed 40 pounds, so the rest of the moose was a heavy load to drag, even across snow. Wolves are so strong that people who maintain them in enclosures are careful to avoid horseplay that would allow the wolves to discover how easily they can overpower humans.

Wolves are extremely hardy. They survive injuries that would kill animals with softer makeups. Half the wolves autopsied in an Alaskan study had suffered at least one major injury, such as a broken rib, leg, or fractured skull. Remember that a broken rib or leg means something different to a wolf than to a dog. No veterinarian is available to treat a busted-up wolf.

The most aggressive wolves in a pack, the ones that initiate attacks on large prey animals, are particularly liable to be injured. The skeleton of one alpha male showed several healed injuries from earlier prey encounters, including several broken ribs (possibly from different encounters), a kicked-out tooth, and a fractured jaw. That wolf was finally killed when a deer drove a hoof through its skull.

A wolf in Minnesota lived for several years on three legs. When researchers caught her, they found that one of her back legs was broken and swinging uselessly. They speculated that she had been hit by a car or a moose. After a veterinarian removed the bad leg, the wolf was released. She not only survived with just one back leg, but went on to make history as one of the principles in the most unusual romantic triangle in wolf research literature. The three-legged female slipped away and had a two-hour "date" with the alpha male of an adjoining pack. To complicate things, her alpha male apparently mated with another female in his pack. Such sexual shenanigans, while common enough with humans, are a kinky rarity among wolves.

THE VITAL WOLF

All the individual senses and abilities of wolves are remarkable enough, yet we underestimate wolves when we examine them piece by piece. The wolf is greater than the sum of its parts. Science hasn't yet found a way to measure the wolf's tenacity and its ferocious will to live.

Wolves lead extremely strenuous lives, often while carrying heavy loads of internal and external parasites. Researchers never touch wolf scat with a bare hand, because of all the parasite eggs likely to be present. Wolves are also capable of fending off a wide range of canine diseases that regularly kill unvaccinated dogs. Wolves have survived gunshots and major injuries that, by any reasonable calculation, should have been fatal.

The vitality of wolves might best be illustrated with a story told by the writer Barry Lopez. While this story may be exaggerated, it says something true about the essential nature of wolves.

An aerial hunter in Alaska once caught ten wolves crossing an open stretch of mountainous terrain. They had no place to hide, so the hunter easily killed nine of the pack. The tenth wolf dashed toward the tip of a spur. Because the hunter knew that the spur ended in a sheer cliff with an enormous drop, he held his fire to see what the wolf would do. Lopez writes: "Without hesitation, the wolf sailed off the spur, fell the 300 feet into a snowbank, and came out running in an explosion of powder."

ARE WOLVES A THREAT TO HUMANS?

Wolf advocates would like to answer this emotionally-charged question with an unequivocal "no." Instead, most are careful enough to repeat the position of such authorities as Dave Mech: "There is no record of an unprovoked, non-rabid wolf in North America seriously injuring a person."

Take note of all those qualifiers:

"unprovoked," "non-rabid," "North America," and "seriously." This is frustrating, for the evidence almost allows us to state flatly that wolves never hurt people.

We know that wolves are less of a threat than bees, many breeds of dogs, bicycles, falling trees, slippery bathtubs, roller-blade skates, and tainted potato salads. Those things all kill people from time to time, whereas wolves never do. Anyone who understands statistics can only marvel at the absurdity of a man who inhales cigarette smoke worrying that he might be attacked by a wolf. Of course, human phobias never correspond to statistics.

Authorities are somewhat divided on the question of whether wolves killed humans in times past. There are so many reports of wolf attacks from Eurasia that it's difficult to dismiss them all. Many sound authentic, and some have been repeated by credible people. But inquiries into such stories come to one of three conclusions: the "wolf" was a wolf-dog hybrid (and hybrids do sometimes attack people); the wolf was rabid; or the story cannot be substantiated (and probably did not happen).

The record in North America is unambiguous. There have been a few aggressive wolf-human contacts but no fatal encounters. Wolves have snapped at people who tried to defend their dogs while wolves were attacking them. One famous encounter involved a Minnesota hunter who had soaked his clothing in deer scent. At dusk when the man, standing within a small opening in dense woods, bent over to tie his snowshoe, a wolf hurtled into him, then dashed away. In a split second, that wolf apparently mistook the confusing shape of the bent-over hunter for what he smelled like: a deer.

Wolves have not lacked opportunities to attack humans. Each year, tens of thousands of people camp in the Boundary Waters Canoe Area Wilderness of northern Minnesota, an area that has always been populated by wolves. Not one person has been attacked or threatened by a wolf. Imagine the odds! Over the years, children must have played within sight of an injured or sick wolf that was hungry to the point of starvation. Yet none has ever attacked.

Two facts can help us understand the wolf's remarkable track record.

First, wolves have learned from bitter experience that humans are the most deadly animal on earth. For many centuries, people have killed wolves at virtually every opportunity. Most wolves make every possible

effort to avoid humans.

Second, people don't present the cues that provoke wolves to attack ungulates. An upright human looks, smells, and moves nothing like a deer. Wolf attacks are usually triggered by the flight of a prey animal, especially if that animal does not move with the fluid grace of a healthy individual. Animals that stand their ground are usually not attacked, and humans usually stand their ground.

Some people who know wolves believe they *might* attack under certain circumstances. A former wolf trapper never feared wolves, except in one situation. "They get pretty brazen," he said, "when you're on the ice." In that setting, a wolf that has not learned to fear humans might be more of a threat than a typical human-fearing wolf. Hypothetically, if such an animal approached a human on the ice . . . and if that person ran like a panicked sheep . . . and if he fled with the herky-jerky motion of an injured animal . . . the wolf might receive enough of the right signals to attack.

On the other hand, it probably wouldn't. Animals do what they have done before, and North America's wolves have never taken advantage of their countless opportunities to attack people. They have not attacked even when provoked by people who were raiding pups from their den.

According to Greek legend, Aeschylus was killed when an eagle dropped a tortoise on the playwright's head from a great height. If true, that makes tortoise-toting eagles more dangerous than North American wolves, as the wolves have yet to kill a single person.

CHAPTER 5

Wolf Society

Wolf experts flinch when they hear someone say, "Wolves always . . ." or "Wolves never . . .." While wolves are orderly creatures that behave according to certain basic principles, they're also flexible and difficult to predict. Wolves are social animals. Much of a wolf's personality and behavior is learned, not genetically fixed as "instinct." This makes wolves less stereotyped in their behavior than many animals. It also makes them fascinating.

THE WOLF PERSONALITY

Generalizing about the "wolf personality" is tricky for several reasons. It's difficult to say which personality characteristics are inherent and which are acquired through learning. Wolves have been described as extremely "shy" and fearful of humans. But some of that shyness might be a response to centuries of persecution. Wolves appear to be losing some of their fear of humans in regions where they have enjoyed pro-

tection under the Endangered Species Act. Most wolves seeing a human still swap ends and vanish. Yet it is becoming more common for a wolf confronting a human to gaze at the person in thoughtful curiosity.

Second, social animals like wolves don't all have the same personality. That only makes sense. After all, dogs—even dogs from the same litter—exhibit wonderfully diverse personalities. Inuit and other native groups have occasionally been amused to discover that a visiting biologist thought all wolves were alike. They aren't.

Third, a wolf's personality changes as the wolf matures and assumes different roles within the pack. Pack leaders are decisive, outgoing, and self-confident. Pack underlings are obsequious and loyal to the leader. Some low-ranking adults are playful and goofy, blending aspects of the adult personality with puppy qualities. But when a low-ranking wolf assumes alpha status, it acquires some

The wolf's society is not always a polite one.

61

version of the classic alpha personality.

With all those qualifications, what can we say about the wolf personality? The key to understanding wolves is understanding the social dynamics of the pack.

For the pack to adhere and function, its members must live cooperatively. A wolf pack is held together by bonds of affection. Adolph Murie wrote, "The strongest impression remaining with me after watching the wolves on numerous occasions was their friendliness." Reunions between pack members are celebrated with a display of joy that has been called the "jubilation of wolves." Anyone who has owned a dog can understand the bonds of loyalty that link pack members. The affection that pack members have for each other is the same "love" that dogs extend to their human families.

Pack members cooperate extensively with each other. Wolves cooperate when hunting, and they spend much of their lives hunting. Low-ranking members sometimes perform "babysitting" chores, and all pack members, even the lordly alphas, may feed the pups. At times, injured wolves have been nurtured by other pack members. In Alaska, a wolf caught in a trap was apparently fed for several days by other pack members. However, this kind of cooperation is atypical.

Conflict within the pack is abnormal and deeply disturbing to wolves. That's hardly surprising, since social discord is incompatible with the efficient functioning of a pack. One of Lois Crisler's wolves was so distressed when it witnessed a dog fight that it separated the combatants, yanking one back by the tail. A good deal of snapping and snarling is common within packs, but serious aggression is not.

Wolves are so docile in certain situations that people have damned them as "cowardly." For example, most wolves caught in leg-hold traps are oddly compliant. A trapper interviewed by Barry Lopez described approaching a wolf in one of his sets. The wolf whined softly and extended the trapped foot, as if requesting help. A retired Minnesota wolf trapper told me, "I never saw a wolf I couldn't trust." By this he meant that trapped wolves accept their doom with dignified composure. "They weren't cowards," he explained. "They just knew they'd had it."

What accounts for this timidity in an animal powerful enough to easily kill a human? Researchers speculate that because wolves live in hierar-

chies, they naturally defer to self-confident humans as they would to an alpha wolf. Wolves may recognize and honor dominance, even in an animal of another species.

Wolves are not sloppy in their social relations. They live in a highly structured social system and take great pains not to upset the integrity of that system. Each wolf knows exactly where it ranks in the pack's pecking order and what actions, accordingly, it may and may not take.

One reason that wolves make inappropriate pets is the fact that few humans are perceptive enough to live with wolves without violating their rules of social discourse. People frequently ignore or misread signals from their pet wolves. These misunderstandings sometimes result in aggressive incidents, which may in turn cause people to kill or dispose of their pets. R.D. Lawrence's book, *In Praise of Wolves*, offers several analyses of complex social interactions involving wolves in confinement.

It's remarkable that wolves are willing to view humans as other wolves. Crisler and her husband were delighted to find that they could communicate with their wolves by adopting wolf body gestures. Lori Schmidt, who maintained a pack of

Each wolf knows exactly where it ranks in the pack's "pecking order."

captive wolves for the International Wolf Center, learned to anticipate which sorts of people would provoke her wolves. "Flaky" people and people with low self-esteem, she says, upset the IWC wolves. R.D. Lawrence was told by a person who often took a leashed wolf into schools that the wolf would occasionally growl quietly at a child. Invariably, said the keeper, the teacher would later identify the child as an outcast who was rejected by other children.

Wolves are usually hostile toward wolves that don't belong to their own pack. Packs often kill lone wolves that trespass into their territory. Turf wars between packs sometimes break out along territorial borders. Bob Cary, a veteran outdoorsman who has lived in wolf country for most of his life, once came upon bloody snow littered with bits of wolf fur. After studying the tracks, Cary determined that four wolves had been trailing a deer when a group of five (probably the resident pack) attacked them. Three of the four trespassers were killed and eaten. This occurred at a time when low deer populations were putting great stress on local wolf populations.

While admirers of wolves are discomfited by this feature of the wolf personality, it is simply another aspect of pack social dynamics. Alien packs and even unattached single wolves represent a threat to a resident pack, so they are often dealt with harshly. In this regard, as in others, wolf packs resemble human street gangs, offering their own members affection and support while exhibiting territorialism, violence, and intolerance toward outsiders. However, recent research suggests that wolves in some areas may be less rigid. One study conducted in Alaska's Denali National Park documented cases of pack-switching among wolves.

The wolves' innate hostility to competitors may explain why they kill coyotes and dogs. Wolves raised with dogs are different; they view the dogs as fellow pack members. But wild wolves encountering a coyote or a dog will often attack it. A bitter joke in the 1960s defined a conservative on the issue of crime as "a liberal who was mugged." Today, some wolf enemies are animal-lovers who have had a beloved pet killed by wolves.

Wolves are usually hostile toward outsiders that don't belong in the pack.

THE PACK

A pack is basically an extended family of wolves. Most packs consist of a dominant breeding pair and any number of their offspring. Of course, it isn't quite that simple; very little about wolves is! Some packs include "aunts and uncles." Occasionally a non-related wolf attaches to a pack. Now and then an alpha wolf lives long enough to be toppled from its throne by a more vigorous pack member. The old wolf remains a pack member, albeit with reduced status.

A wolf pack is not a loose collection of animals, but a tightly knit, organized group. Pack members stay together much of the time, usually hunting and defending territory together. Some researchers feel that pack structure is tightest in winter. This makes sense, as winter is a difficult season for wolves—a time when efficient hunting and stout territorial defense are badly needed.

Biologists use names for different classes of pack members. The cocky, happy leaders who do the breeding in

A wolf pack is a tightly knit, organized group.

a pack are the "alphas." Adults rank-ing below the alphas are sometimes called "biders," because they are bid-ing their time, waiting to advance in rank. In large packs, some unfortu-nate animal may become the scapegoat or "omega" wolf that must tolerate abuse from all other pack members. The pups occupy a special position that is not, strictly speaking, above or below the omega wolves.

There are two lines of dominance, one male and one female. The alpha male enforces the male dominance line and the alpha female enforces the female line. The alpha female is particularly aggressive in defending her exclusive right to breed. Among wolves (including red wolves), there are several documented cases of mothers killing daughters in fights over access to the breeding male.

Wolves engage in many small acts of dominance that reinforce the clari-ty of the pecking order. Dominant wolves pick on lower animals at odd moments, for no apparent reason except to demonstrate that they have the right to do so. Many of these tests come at eating time. While the seem-ingly gratuitous displays of superiority look nasty to humans, they prevent

more dangerous conflicts that could result from ambiguity about status. Few of the people who believe that wolves are morally superior to humans would enjoy life as a low-ranking member of a wolf pack.

Researchers no longer claim that packs are always led by males, or even that a pack typically has a single leader. In many situations, such as choosing a route or deciding to attack a prey animal, one wolf clearly leads. Most observers have assumed that this is the alpha male. But at times, the alpha female dominates the male, so leadership is shared. Packs usually respect the wishes of leaders, although Dave Mech once observed a leader abandon a plan that was unpopular with the pack.

Packs can number as few as two wolves or as many as 30. Most packs in the continental U.S. number between five and ten. In Alaska and northern Canada, packs frequently number between ten and 20. A pack in Glacier Park recently included 20 animals—unusually large for the continental U.S. The group eventually split into two packs that were unusually tolerant of each other, visiting each other's territory without conflict. The alpha female of one pack was the mother of the breeding female in the second, which might explain the absence of territorial conflict.

A pack changes size throughout the year. It achieves maximum size in late fall, when a fresh cohort of pups joins the hunt. The pack dwindles to its nadir in early spring, when its numbers are depleted by winter mortality and the defection of young wolves that seek their fortunes apart from the pack.

Pack coherence is dynamic rather than static. Life in a pack offers individual wolves certain survival advantages, particularly when it comes to killing large prey animals. Wolves are strongly motivated to stay within their packs by those benefits plus the emotional "glue" that bonds pack members to each other. Yet all pack members below the alphas must sacrifice self-interest to live in the pack. They constantly defer to the alphas in such matters as breeding rights and access to food. To some extent, self-interest and group unity are in conflict; thus there are always centrifugal and centripetal forces acting on a pack. When the pack grows too large, stress sets in, the center no longer holds, and the pack splits.

Pack size seems related to prey size, although the connection is not a neat one. Wolves that prey on small animals typically live in small groups of

Dominant wolves may pick on other pack members for no apparent reason.

two wolves. Wolves that prey mostly on deer usually form packs of four to six animals. Wolves preying on such sizeable and dangerous animals as moose need the cooperation of several good hunters, so wolf packs in moose country are large. Yet, after a pack numbers five or six adult wolves, adding members provides no hunting advantage . . . and that confuses the issue. The relationship between prey and pack size might have less to do with killing than dining: Large packs more efficiently consume large prey, and small packs more efficiently consume small prey.

COMMUNICATION

A social animal cannot afford fuzzy communications. For example, a wolf must be able to discriminate between a bluff and a genuine status challenge. While wolves cannot make speeches or send faxes, they make themselves understood quite clearly with a combination of vocalizations, body postures, and scents.

Wolves growl, squeal, bark, whine, and, of course, howl. Whimpering or whining conveys friendly intentions. Crisler was probably referring to whimpering when she described her wolves "talking." She wrote, "The wolf talking is deeply impressive, because the wolf is so emotionally stirred. His eyes are brilliant with feeling." Growling is a threatening noise. Barks signal alarm.

Wolf howls are one of the most moving and haunting sounds in nature. An old trapper described a pack howl as "a dozen train whistles braided together." The first time I heard wolves howl, I was camping in a canoe wilderness, sleeping in a nylon tent that suddenly seemed thin and insubstantial. Though I knew I was in no danger, that lugubrious moaning in the darkness made my hair stand up in places where I hadn't known I had hair.

Wolves throw themselves into howling with evident joy. Crisler compared howling to "a community sing." She wrote, "Wolves love a howl. When it is started, they instantly seek contact with one another, troop together, fur to fur. Some wolves . . . will run from any distance, panting and bright-eyed, to join in, uttering, as they near, fervent little wows, jaws wide, hardly able to wait to sing."

Each howling wolf sings a unique note. When Crisler howled with her wolves she learned that if she trespassed on the note a wolf was singing, it would instantly shift up or down by a note or two. "Wolves avoid unison singing," Crisler concluded. "They like chords." Possibly, but biologists believe the function of polyphonic singing is to increase vocal impact. Wolves singing two different notes produce three tones—the two being sung plus a harmonic. Fred Harrington, a researcher who did extensive work with howling, noted that an observer can distinguish between one and two howling wolves, but "any more than two sound like a dozen."

Ulysses S. Grant and his guide once heard a stirring chorus of wolf

Each howling wolf sings a unique note.

howls. The guide asked how many animals were making the sound. Grant foolishly decided to prove that he was no dude. Although he was certain that so much sound could only be produced by a huge pack, Grant said that just 20 wolves were howling. The men soon rode up upon the pack. Two wolves sat on their haunches, howling with open mouths held close together like barbershop quartet singers.

Howling celebrates and reinforces pack unity. In that regard, wolves resemble such human packs as street gangs and athletic teams, which have their own solidarity rituals. It is accurate—though a little fanciful—to translate some group howls as meaning something like: "We're the Mink Lake pack, and we're alright! Trespassers here are in for a fight!"

Like "aloha," the howl of a wolf has several meanings, and which one applies is determined by context. Wolves howl to reinforce territorial claims, particularly when challenged by the howls of an intruding pack. Fred Harrington concluded that wolves howl most readily when they have something to defend, like pups in a den or a fresh kill. Pack members howl back and forth to keep track of each other when visual communication isn't possible. A howling session can reunite a pack that has broken up to hunt within an area. Sometimes a pack howls after making a kill. This may be a device to keep alien packs away from the kill, or it might be the wolf equivalent of the "high fives"—jubilant gestures used by athletes following a big score.

Wolves respond to human howls. Researchers often howl to trigger a reply that confirms a pack's presence in a certain area. Wisconsin wolf biologist Adrian Wydeven monitored one remarkable old male wolf nicknamed "Whistler" for many years. During a fall howl census, Wydeven got a response from Whistler's territory. But something was wrong. "I don't want to anthropomorphize, but the howl was low and distinctive. To me, it sounded lonely. We were concerned because we knew that pack had at least three pups in spring, but now there was just one adult. Whistler went on howling for 35 minutes. When I left he was still howling, still sounding lonely." Weeks later, Wydeven howled at the same location, and was thrilled to hear a chorus from a whole pack, soprano puppy squeals mixed in with the bass notes of Whistler and his mate. Apparently the pack was reunited.

The willingness of wolves to howl

back at people has created a curious sort of tourism. Many groups and agencies now sponsor howling trips to known pack locations. After all, howling is about the only way in which a person who's fascinated by wolves can experience direct contact with a wild wolf. It's thrilling to howl into the darkness of a wilderness area and listen as a wolf answers you. Of course, the wolf may be saying something like, "Buzz off, dammit!" But it is, nonetheless, talking to you.

Body language and facial gestures help wolves maintain the pecking order. The faces of most wolves are tinted in ways that highlight their changing expressions. For example, the black lips contrast with the white teeth and the creamy light fur. Like mimes, wolves have plastic, variable faces that dramatize their changing emotions in ways that even humans can understand.

Various body postures allow wolves to convey messages. A wolf saying "hello" drops its head to the ground, exposing its vulnerable neck in a gesture of submission. Dominant wolves intimidate lesser pack members with fixed stares. In wolf society, making eye contact is aggressive posturing, not good manners. Wolves also express dominance by such gestures as standing up to ride across the back of another wolf.

A wolf's tail is the semaphore that signals its attitude. High tails indicate dominance and high spirits, although there are fine nuances of tail height and position that allow a wolf to communicate specific messages. Submissive animals tuck their tails tightly under their bellies. Even untrained observers can spot dominant and submissive wolves by noting tail postures.

Scent is the wolves' third medium for social interchange. Scientists know less about scent because, unlike other forms of discourse, humans cannot perceive scent directly. Its function must be inferred by watching wolves respond.

Alpha males and females raise their legs to urinate, spraying scent up high where it will be conspicuous. Lesser pack members of both sexes squat like female dogs when urinating. Urine depositions mark the boundaries of a pack's territory. Like the spray-painted graffiti used by a street gang, these "Keep Out!" signs are particularly dense where territorial boundaries are close together.

Scent helps wolves navigate through their territories. Wolves leave scent-marks at significant points, such as trail junctions, creating olfactory points of reference.

Wolves have "mental maps" that allow them to beeline cross-country and find their destination.

Trappers used to believe that wolves moved around their territories in rigid patterns; some thought they they always moved clockwise, for example. Researchers now know that wolves retain superb mental maps that allow them to leave a familiar trail and bee-line cross-country to a particular destination.

Other uses of scent are more obscure. Wolves often defecate near such man-made objects as aluminum cans. Wolf trappers hated finding piles of dung beside their exquisitely disguised trap sets, because the wolves seem to be mocking their professional skills. A more plausible interpretation is that the dung simply marks a dangerous object for the benefit of other pack members.

TERRITORY

Territorialism is not understood as well as some other aspects of wolf biology, mostly because it's difficult and expensive to study. Many research assistants must monitor many wolves wearing collars over long periods of time in order to learn where the wolves do and do not go. This research might in the future be conducted using radio collars monitored by satellites, although neither the collars nor the satellites are very cheap.

People often assume that wolf territories are as rigidly bordered as nation states. The image is misleading. Territories sometimes overlap. More often, adjacent territories are not contiguous, like national borders, but are separated by "buffer zones."

Territorial borders also fluctuate, changing size as packs change size. There may even be a seasonal dimension to territories, meaning that habitat defended by a pack in February might not bear defending in June. Like so many aspects of wolf society, territories are subject to constant revision.

It's clear that wolves need a lot of living space. Whereas a deer might live in a territory of less than half a square mile, most wolf packs defend territories of 50 to 150 square miles. The smallest area that can serve a pack in good deer country is 30 square miles, whereas packs in Arctic areas must hunt territories as large as 1,000 square miles.

Bob Cary, a long-time observer of wolves, describes wolf territories in northeastern Minnesota as "like Swiss cheese," with the holes representing established territories and the cheese signifying buffer zones. Prey animals concentrate in the buffer zones. Cary has learned that his chance of bagging a deer for his family improves if he hunts the cheese and avoids the holes.

CHAPTER 6

The Year of the Wolf

The wolf's year breaks down into two rather different halves. During most of the fall and winter, the pack lives on the run. In spring and summer, the pack has a more or less fixed address while it concentrates on raising a new generation of wolves.

The annual pattern described here applies to most—but not all—wolves. Some wolves that prey upon caribou, for example, have evolved a different lifestyle, following the great herds as they migrate.

THE PANTRY

The wolf's reproductive cycle is synchronized to take advantage of seasonal food abundance. Wolves prey primarily on ungulates. Deer and moose typically have a hard time in winter. They enter the spring in poor condition, making them vulnerable to wolves at just the time when wolves need a reliable source of nutrition for their pups.

Denning wolves must do all of their hunting in a limited area, rather

than roving widely as they do the rest of the year. Only in summer can the food resources of a single area sustain the growing pack. Most ungulates give birth early in summer. The newborn moose, caribou, and deer are vulnerable to predation. Thus the wolves' pantry is restocked with a fresh bounty of young caribou, moose, and deer each summer.

The bounty doesn't last. As wolves and other predators make repeated withdrawals from the supply of prey animals, finding food becomes more of a challenge. The pantry gets bare as winter winds onward. For wolves, winter is the cruel filter—the time in which life's winners and losers are sorted.

DISPERSERS

Now and then, a young wolf decides to strike off on its own. A bider, in other words, elects to become a disperser. Most dispersers are yearlings, and both sexes are known to disperse.

These defections from the pack are

The wolf's year breaks down into two distinct halves.

remarkable. Wolves are social animals, so a lone wolf is a wolf living unnaturally. It must be difficult for the wolf to sever the emotional bonds that have held it within the pack. Some dispersers need to work up to the break by undertaking a series of short experiments with independence.

Dispersing also exposes wolves to great hazards. Acquiring food is difficult and dangerous even for a pack, so a lone wolf hunts at an enormous disadvantage. Dispersers risk being

In the weeks before mating, breeding wolves begin to groom and fondle each other.

attacked for trespassing on the territories of other wolf packs. For all these reasons, mortality among dispersers is high.

Why disperse, if doing so is risky and difficult? Some young wolves simply get fed up with low pack status. In particular, they may resent being denied the right to breed. Researchers think it's significant that dispersers often leave shortly before the mating season, a time of high tension within the pack. In other words, young wolves leave packs for about the same reasons that maturing humans reject the confining comfort of their parents' homes.

No single pattern applies to all dispersers. Some remain within their former pack's territory. Others take off on a line, as if they had a compass, a map, and a distant destination in mind. Dispersers can move astonishing distances. A few have traveled over 500 miles before finding what they were seeking. Other dispersers drift into the buffer zones between pack territories. Now and then, a dispersing wolf encounters a resident pack and becomes accepted as a member.

Dispersing wolves search for unoccupied territory and an unattached wolf of the opposite sex. Some succeed in both objectives, although many more do not. Researchers generally believe that such a happy meeting of two dispersers is the main way in which wolves form new packs.

The mechanism of dispersal ensures that wolves make the best use of their habitat. When conditions are favorable (that is, when food is abundant), dispersers survive and form new packs; when conditions are unfavorable, dispersers die. Dispersing may also minimize the genetic problems that could arise from inbreeding.

Researchers would like to know more about these bold young wolves. How do they differ from siblings that elect to continue as biders within the pack? Are dispersers particularly capable, self-confident, or sexually driven individuals?

COURTSHIP AND REPRODUCTION

Each year, a wolf pack must renew its claim on the future by offsetting attrition through reproduction. But since overpopulation is as threatening to wolves as inadequate fertility, several devices limit the animal's reproductive potential.

Wolves do not usually reach sexual maturity and reproduce until they are three, four, or five years old. Some wolves reproduce when they're two years old, and a few zoo wolves have done so when just a year old, but wild wolves generally need more time to become sexually mature. Wolves apparently mature earlier when prey is abundant, when the pack has suffered high mortality, or when abundant habitat makes dispersal and early breeding a workable strategy. The variable age of sexual maturity is one of the shock absorbers that keep wolf numbers aligned with the capacity of the territory to support them.

The main limitation on reproduction is social. The alpha male denies other males access to the breeding female, and she prevents other females from associating with the alpha male. As a result, most packs produce just a single litter.

Some packs include a second

breeding female and thus a second litter of pups. Pups from the second litter don't enjoy the same prospects as the alpha pair's pups, but if food is plentiful, many pups from the second litter may survive. Second litters are another way in which wolf numbers are adjusted in accordance with the food resources of their habitat.

In the weeks before mating, the breeding pair engages in a number of affectionate gestures, grooming and fondling each other. Less romantically, the breeding pair performs "RLUs" (raised leg urinations). When the female is in estrus, her urine is bloody. Researchers who monitor wolf populations look for double urine marks in the winter snow. The marks represent the promise that another litter of wolf pups will soon be nuzzling the mother's teats in a nearby den.

The mating season can be protracted over a period of weeks in late winter or spring. Northern wolves mate later than southern wolves, probably because northern ungulates produce their offspring later in the year. Breeding couples sometimes slip away from the pack to copulate in private. They aren't modest. They simply need to get away from pesky, non-breeding wolves.

Very little about wolf biology is cut-and-dried. Sometimes the alpha male or alpha female does not choose to participate in breeding. Nobody knows why. Mated pairs are usually faithful to each other while both partners survive, but not always. As mentioned earlier, wolves have been known to conduct illicit affairs. Irregular sexual behavior might be more common than is now known, for few packs have been studied intensively enough to document deviances.

After breeding, the female seeks a den. Old den sites are often used year after year, and some have been used continuously for many decades. The den Murie observed in Alaska is still producing young wolves today, more than 50 years later. If a female cannot find a suitable den, she digs one. Or

Wolf pups are winsome creatures that have melted the hearts of wolf trappers.

she evicts some smaller animal from its home and enlarges the domicile to suit her needs.

Dens are usually caves, holes in the ground, or chambers formed by a jumble of large rocks. A den must be dry and secure, situated in good hunting territory, and located near water. Wolves prefer den sites near high ground, so they can survey their surroundings as they loaf. While lounging in elevated areas may help wolves spot approaching danger, researchers also believe that wolves simply prefer a scenic view while they're resting.

PUPS

Wolf pups are born 63 days after the breeding pair mates. Litters range in size from three to nine pups, but most consist of four to six. The pug-nosed pups are born blind, deaf, and capable of only a limited amount of scooting around in order to stay near the warmth of their mother. Pups weigh about a pound at birth but grow rapidly. Once they hit their growth stride, wolf pups can gain three pounds per week.

At several weeks of age, young wolves are so winsome that they have melted the hearts of men who make

their livelihood by killing wolves. One wolfer wrote, "I have never had to do anything that goes against the grain more than to kill the pups at this stage. Potential murderers they may be, but at this time they are just plump, friendly little things that nuzzle you and whine little pleased whines."

At about three weeks, the pups begin venturing into the outside world. They romp at the den mouth and begin play-fighting. At this age, little wolves form bonds with the rest of the pack. Pups raised by humans at this stage will bond to people instead of wolves. Similarly, people who breed dogs know that there's a critical time period during which the puppies must be exposed to humans. If this doesn't happen, the pups grow into adults that never completely accept and trust people.

All pack members involve themselves with the wolf pups. Even the alpha male usually exhibits tolerance for their tomfoolery. In zoos, some unbred female wolves undergo the hormonal changes of pregnancy, in what is called a "pseudo pregnancy," later producing milk and nursing the pups. Wet-nursing has not been confirmed among wild wolves, but it may exist. Low-ranking pack members often become "aunts" and "uncles" with special bonds to the pups.

At about three weeks, pups begin to explore the outside world.

Wolves introduce pups to solid food in an ingenious way. Each day, pack members radiate out from the den to hunt, while the mother remains behind to care for her offspring. Successful hunters fill up with meat, then return to the den, where they disgorge a meal for the pups and the nursing mother. The disgorged food provides the pups with tenderized, chopped-up meat that their digestive systems can handle. Later on, pack members bring undigested meat, like a deer haunch, to the pups.

Starting very early in life, little wolves engage in endless hours of roughhousing. All the pouncing, stalking, and fighting serves two critical functions. The pups are acquiring skills they will use to hunt real prey in a few months. At the same time, they're establishing their own dominance hierarchy.

When the pups reach about nine weeks of age, they're mobile enough to permit the pack to move to a "rendezvous site." Dave Mech describes these as "essentially a den above ground." Rendezvous sites are secure areas near water, where the pups can cavort in safety while the rest of the pack hunts. Some rendezvous sites are used year after year, like dens. If the pack makes a kill, the adults may move the pups to the kill site rather than the other way around—another way of creating a rendezvous site.

Sometime in early fall, the pack hits the trail again with the pups running along. Though the youngsters are now full-sized and look like adults, they can do little more than cheerlead during attacks on prey until they become a year old. The first year of life is a harsh form of schooling. Young wolves that fail to receive passing grades are not alive for long.

CHAPTER 7

Wolves and Their Prey

It seems so simple: Surround a deer, cut it down with a few bites, then *bon appetit!*

But for wolves, acquiring food is anything but easy. While an animal that eats browse or grass can just about count on eating every day, wolves frequently go several days between meals. Sometimes the gap stretches to weeks.

NO DAINTY EATER

Wolves do indeed "wolf" their food. Four wolves once consumed most of a mule deer in four hours. A wolf can bolt down a meal of 18 pounds of meat—the equivalent of a man devouring a 40-pound steak—at one sitting. Hungry wolves eat until their bellies are stretched to the limit, lie down to digest for several hours, then get up and do it all over again. Old-time wolf hunters knew it was relatively easy to sneak up on logy, "meat-drunk" wolves.

The wolf's digestive system is adapted for processing food quickly.

Because its metabolism runs at such a hot pace, a wolf must drink copious amounts of water to avoid uremic poisoning. That's one reason den sites and wolf travelways are usually near water.

Wolves consume as much of their prey as they can. They usually leave behind only a few scraps of hide, the skull, the backbone, and perhaps the stomach contents. After a kill, the pack either camps at the site or revisits the carcass until even the bony lower legs have been eaten. When a pack abandons a kill, almost nothing remains to indicate that an animal weighing as much as 1,000 pounds was consumed at a site.

In the process of devouring their prey, wolves swallow large amounts of bone and hair. It would seem that splintered bones would hazardous to consume. After all, veterinarians now counsel dog owners to avoid feeding bones to their pets because sharp bones can puncture soft stomach or intestinal walls. But in a wolf's

---

The most dramatic moment in the hunt occurs when prey and predator make eye contact.

stomach and intestines, sharp objects are wrapped in hair until the package resembles a furry cocoon.

This explains the bizarre story about the wolf scat that was found to contain a Mepps Spinner. The Mepps is a popular fishing lure that carries an unusually sharp treble hook. Because that fishing lure was encased in a mass of felt-like hair, it passed through the wolf without incident.

Okay, but how did a fishing lure get into a wolf? Researchers have a strong hunch. The wolf that excreted the spinner was a female with a den near a great blue heron rookery. In her travels, she frequently swung by the rookery to check under the trees for food. Researchers assume that a fish hit an angler's spinner and broke the line. The fish was then probably picked up by a heron. Perhaps the heron ate the fish, died, and was eaten by the wolf. Even more likely, the heron ate the fish but kicked the head out of the nest. The wolf then might have eaten the fish head, spinner and all.

WHAT THEY EAT

Wolves aren't fussy eaters, although they are definitely carnivorous. They'll consume almost any meat they can acquire, including birds, fish, hares, lizards, mice, insects, and worms. The fact that wolves eat maggoty carrion suggests that their energy budget is too stringent to let them bypass an easy meal, even if that meal is spoiled.

A common interest in carrion might explain the odd partnership that exists between wolves and ravens. Ravens follow wolves to feed on their kills. In fact, a good way to locate wolves is to look under a raven flock. But the relationship is not one-sided. With their great intelligence, sharp eyes, and aerial perspective, ravens can alert wolves to danger. Ravens may also guide wolves to carrion.

Yet there is more to the wolf-raven relationship than mutual nutritional benefits. Wolves and ravens sometimes play games with each other. Some individual ravens and wolves seem to develop genuine friendships. After all, wolves and ravens are the two most social and intelligent species in northern ecosystems. It makes some sense that they take pleasure in each other's company.

Large ungulates are the most suitable prey for wolves. Wolves mainly prey on deer, moose, caribou, elk, sheep, and musk-oxen. The length of that list is misleading, for only one or two ungulate species are likely to live within any pack's territory.

Because they hunt in packs, wolves need a sizable meal, but that doesn't mean small animals are never important in the wolf diet. Beavers and hares might play a critical role by providing nutrition at a time of year when it is especially needed. Wolves rarely hunt prey smaller than beavers. Any mousing they engage in is casual, and is probably motivated more by boredom than hunger.

Wolves aren't fussy eaters.

PREDATOR-PREY RELATIONS

One of the most complicated and controversial aspects of wolf biology is the impact wolves have on prey species. Over time, research on this topic has changed emphasis. Early research emphasized how difficult it is for wolves to catch healthy ungulates. Later research has shown wolves to be adaptable predators that are capable

of surviving even in difficult times. Research on predator-prey relations is greatly complicated by differences in geography, climate, the species compositions of the predator-prey systems, and whether humans are also part of the system.

In general, wolves cannot kill whenever they choose. They traverse large territories and hunt vigorously to find enough food to sustain themselves. It has to be that way. Any predator capable of killing at will would decimate its own food supply and quickly become a footnote in evolutionary history. For a predator-prey system to function over time, parity must exist between the eater and the eaten.

And it does. Deer are usually too alert to be approached and too quick to be caught, once they bolt. Moose sometimes outrun wolves and sometimes fight them off with flailing hooves that strike like sledge hammers. Caribou, even the calves, can usually outrun wolves. Sheep and goats use rocky, mountainous terrain to avoid attacks. Musk-oxen form circles of defense that present attacking wolves with a formidable array of wicked horns and hooves.

Yet wolves survive. One way they survive is by traveling mile after mile until they locate a vulnerable animal.

This is why wolf ranges are so large. Putting it the other way around, wolves wouldn't range so far if they were capable of catching a large share of the healthy prey animals they encounter.

Prey animals become vulnerable in a number of ways. Some suffer from arthritis, disease, parasites, or injury. Some prey animals are unwary, slow, or indecisive when attacked. Very old and very young animals are especially vulnerable to predators. Sometimes a harsh winter will make whole populations of ungulates too weak to escape, and under these circumstances wolves may kill more animals than they're able to eat at the time.

All this does not mean that wolves can't catch healthy animals. Sometimes they can, although the odds favor the prey unless it's weakened in one way or another. Wolves cannot afford to waste endless amounts of energy chasing healthy animals. They concentrate their hunting on individuals they're likely to catch.

Many animals killed by wolves would have died even if wolves had not come along. When researchers examine wolf kills they find that a remarkably high percentage of the victims had skeletal deformities or injuries, which means that they were

A kill scene such as the one shown is a sure indication of recent wolf presence.

already in trouble when the wolves found them. By weeding out sick and parasitic animals, wolves might benefit healthy members of ungulate populations. By culling the stupid and slow animals from ungulate herds, wolves ensure that only the fittest live to pass on their genes.

All of this is summed up in the concept of "balance of nature." The basic idea holds that predator species and prey species exist in equilibrium. Wolves control deer numbers by preying on the weakest individuals, and the deer control wolf numbers by being difficult to catch.

Yet things aren't entirely so simple. The balance of predator and prey populations can be upset by several factors—especially by unusual weather patterns. In any particular predator-prey system at any given moment, it's not only possible but likely that the balance will not fit the theoretical ideal. There are often too many predators or too many ungulates. Things balance out over time, but the time lag can be lengthy.

THE HUNT

A wolf on the move is probably always hungry and probably always hunting. And wolves are on the move about eight hours of every day. Sometimes pack members lope along in single file, particularly when

Writer Barry Lopez suggests that a prey animal gives wolves permission to take its life.

they're hunting in snow. At other times, packs fan out to cover more ground and improve the odds of flushing up a victim.

Sooner or later, a pack member will see or smell an animal that might be prey. The pack then becomes excited, although each wolf exercises restraint, moving forward with silent caution. Past experience has taught the wolves that they must close the distance before they can launch a successful attack. Wolves know better than to howl when stalking prey.

The most dramatic moment in the hunt occurs when prey and predator finally make eye contact. Wolves learn much by studying the response of their intended meal. Healthy, self-confident prey animals either flee or take a stand. Weak prey animals give signals that betray their vulnerability. Somehow, wolves can discriminate between the old bull moose that stands its ground because it can't run and the young bull that stands because it doesn't need to run.

Writer Barry Lopez has written somewhat romantically about the moment when predator and prey study each other. Lopez calls this the "conversation of death." In effect, the wolf asks its prey, "Are you ready to die today?" The reply of a vigorous animal is "Hell, no!" But some animals cannot manage such a firm denial. Their body language reflects confusion, fear, weakness. Then the wolf presses the issue. Lopez even suggests that the prey animal gives permission for the wolves to take its life.

Biologists are more comfortable speaking of this encounter as a "testing" process. Testing often involves harassing prey animals to make them run. Injured, weak, or panicky animals betray their vulnerability. Wolves have an uncanny ability to detect the one caribou in a stampeding ocean that isn't running as fluidly as the others.

Lopez's "conversation of death" helps make sense of some cases of livestock depredation. Wolves sometimes run amok among livestock, slaughtering more animals than they could possibly eat. Centuries of domestication have turned livestock animals—which were once wild species—into dependent creatures with few natural instincts and poor mechanisms for coping with predators. When wolves challenge them, sheep and cattle often panic, displaying the signals of wild animals that are distressed and unfit.

Wolves almost always chase animals that run. Running implies weakness, and exposes the animal's vulnerable rump. An animal that holds its ground and maintains eye contact can stop a wolf pack in its tracks, although a small ungulate like a deer cannot stare down a wolf pack indefinitely.

During the initial rush, both the wolf and the prey reach for all the speed they can command. Most prey animals are quick enough to escape. Wolves make remarkably fast decisions about how likely their attack is to pay off. Their energy budget provides little allowance for long, fruitless chases. They persist in long chases only when they have detected some hint of weakness. Wolves become extremely persistent when they have drawn blood. In prolonged fights, a few wolves might take turns harassing and tiring the wounded animal while other pack members rest.

Some hunts take a different course due to special circumstances. Moose, musk-oxen and elk calves are vigorously defended by their mothers. When hunting such calves, a wolf pack concentrates on separating the calf from its defender. Animals chased by wolves often run into water, where they make a stand or swim away to safety. If they can, wolves race around the shoreline to meet the swimmer when it tries to leave the water.

Many winter kills take place on the ice, where wolves clearly have an advantage because they can maneuver better than their prey. Researchers aren't sure whether wolves intentionally drive their prey toward ice. Perhaps some prey animals run to ice, not understanding that frozen lakes are different and vastly more dangerous than open water.

Moose-wolf encounters are interesting because moose are the most dangerous common prey of wolves. While most prey species depend on escaping, a healthy moose can usually fight off a wolf pack. Sometimes a bold wolf will grab the moose's nose. Such a grip is apparently painful, which is perhaps why intransigent bull cattle can be handled by nose rings. A wolf with a good nose grip can often immobilize a moose, allowing the rest of the pack to swarm at its belly and hindquarters. In one moose-wolf fight observed by Dave Mech, a wolf attached itself to the moose's nose so firmly that the moose swung the wolf around in the air.

Research has refuted two myths about the wolf's hunting methods.

Contrary to common belief, wolves do not deliberately hamstring ungulates. Because the hooves are the ungulates' most dangerous weapons, wolves would routinely get their heads kicked if they tried to dive around the hooves to sever tendons. Wolves usually attack high on an animal's rump—a big target and a safe place to bite. If a wolf can sink its long canines into that meaty rump, it can open a wound and perhaps knock the animal off its feet.

Nor is it true that wolves use elaborate strategies in attacking prey. Most chases involve a straightforward pursuit, with no decoys or ambushes. The issue is usually settled by speed and by how close the wolves are able to come before they're detected by their prey. There is one possible exception. Observers have occasionally seen wolves working caribou herds with what appear to be more sophisticated tactics, such as driving caribou toward a wolf pre-positioned for ambush.

Biologists know they're jeered by their peers when they anthropomor-phize, so I'll say what many of them think but won't say: Wolves love to hunt. Of course, a hungry wolf knows it must hunt in order to eat, but the emotional experience of seeking, pursuing, and killing prey must surely be thrilling in its own right. Imagine being a wolf on the hunt, trotting mile after mile through a moonlit forest until you hit that ribbon of breeze freighted with the intoxicating scent of an upwind deer. Imagine the stalk, the tension, the glorious sprint toward the bounding animal, the flying snow, the dangerous leap with snapping teeth, the hot blood steaming in the snow.

The joy of the hunt must be all the more satisfying because it's done in partnership with the rest of the pack. And after making a successful kill, it's easy to understand why a wolf would want to sit down, throw its head back, and . . . howl.

CHAPTER 8

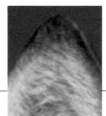

The Enigmatic Red Wolf

In 1624, eight years after his life was spared by the entreaties of young Pocahontas, Captain John Smith published *A General History of Virginia*. The founder of the Roanoke settlement observed, "The wolves are not much bigger than our English fox." Smith was probably the first European to describe the red wolf (*Canis rufus*), the enigmatic wild canid of the American Southeast. He didn't seem to doubt that it was a wolf.

People have often doubted the designation since that time. Nothing about the red wolf has caused so much scientific confusion as its identity. Is it a wolf? If so, how does it differ from the gray wolf? Is it the sole survivor of a primitive race of wolves, or is the red wolf in fact a wolf-coyote hybrid?

These are not esoteric questions.

If you are a biologist struggling to save the last red wolves on earth, you worry about what a red wolf is because you need to decide which of

the animals in your pens are wolves and which are wolf-coyote hybrids.

If you are a lawyer for the American sheep industry, you argue in court that the U.S. Fish & Wildlife Service (FWS) should not treat the red wolf as an endangered species because it isn't a species.

If you are an FWS manager, the issue is nettlesome because your agency isn't supposed to promote the spread of hybrids.

The red wolf is even more interesting because it's the first animal to make the transition from zoo animal to free-ranging predator, and it's the first carnivore ever reestablished in a range where it had become extinct. Efforts to save the red wolf led managers to invent a set of techniques that might soon help restore the northern Rocky Mountain wolf to Yellowstone Park and the Mexican wolf to the Southwest.

The red wolf looks like a wolf-coyote hybrid. Adult coyotes weigh 20 to 50 pounds, adult gray wolves 70 to

---

Scientists have debated: Is the red wolf a wolf, or is it in fact a wolf-coyote hybrid?

Original and Current Range of the Red Wolf

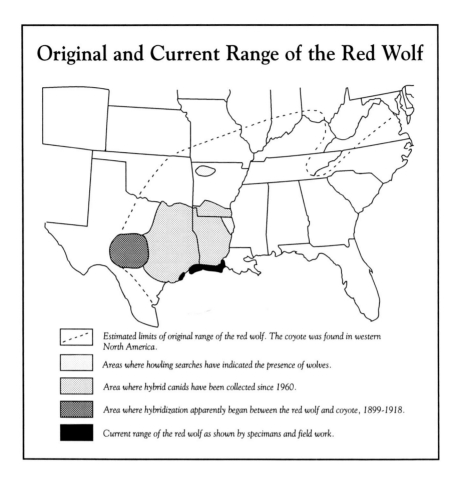

Estimated limits of original range of the red wolf. The coyote was found in western North America.

Areas where howling searches have indicated the presence of wolves.

Area where hybrid canids have been collected since 1960.

Area where hybridization apparently began between the red wolf and coyote, 1899-1918.

Current range of the red wolf as shown by specimans and field work.

110 pounds. At 50 to 80 pounds, the red wolf neatly splits the difference. The red wolf has a short coat, noticeably large ears, very long legs, a delicate frame, and a thin face that carries a narrow snout. While the red wolf lacks the majesty of the gray wolf, many red wolves have a lovely copper coat flecked with dark guard hairs. The coats of red wolves are short-haired compared to those of gray wolves, which enhances the impression of delicacy.

Red wolves living on the northern borders of their range resembled the nearby gray wolves, while red wolves living on the western end of their range resembled nearby coyotes. It should have been the other way around; when similar species live in abutting ranges, morphological differences are usually exaggerated, not minimized. Biologists traditionally sought to define the red wolf's by analyzing skeletal measurements. But that is uncertain science at best. When researchers recently conducted sophisticated genetic tests on DNA taken from red wolves, their inconclusive findings did more to heat up the debate than to resolve it.

Prominent wolf biologists at a 1992 symposium decided to maintain the red wolf's status as a distinct species. A strong argument for that position comes from paleontological studies indicating that red wolves hunted the North American continent at least three-quarters of a million years ago. According to Gary Henry, coordinator of the FWS red wolf program, "If it is a hybrid, the red wolf is a 750,000-year-old hybrid." Henry believes that red wolves and coyotes evolved from an ancient North American canid.

If taxonomist Ron Nowak's analysis is accepted, red wolves assume an intriguing role as the original wolf. Nowak has suggested that red wolves (or a very similar progenitor) evolved from coyotes, and gray wolves later evolved from red wolves. In this analysis, the red wolf is not an illegitimate half-breed but the first true wolf,

a Founding Father of the wolf line.

Many managers argue that the red wolf should be restored even if its status as a species is open to question. For many centuries, the red wolf occupied an important niche in the ecological community of the American Southeast. That niche has gone unfilled since wolves were eradicated. In the words of Curtis Carley, one of the founders of the FWS red wolf recovery program, "Whatever the red wolf is, the wolves we have in captivity seem to breed true and represent the southeastern canine that has been recorded as part of our past." Any animal that has been part of an ecosystem for 750,000 years has a strong presumptive case for belonging in that ecosystem.

THE RED WOLF

The red wolf once ranged over much of the southeastern quarter of the U.S. It lived as far west as central Texas and as far north as southern Illinois. In effect, the red wolf was the top canine predator of the southeastern forests, occupying the niche filled by coyotes in the West and gray wolves in the North.

Little is known about the habits of red wolves in the wild. By the time scientists took an interest in the 1960s, it was too late to begin field studies of the red wolf. The few remaining wolves were struggling to survive in wretched, atypical habitat, their social structures warped by the twin stresses of persecution and severely depressed population levels. Much of what biologists now know about the species comes from studies done on the first generations of red wolves reintroduced into the wild.

Red wolves primarily prey on medium-sized mammals. Common prey animals include grouse and other birds, nutria (an exotic animal that looks like an overgrown muskrat), raccoons, feral pigs, rabbits and hares, squirrels, and deer. When the first wolves released into the wild began hunting their own food, raccoons were a dietary mainstay. Since then, red wolves have become adept at preying on Virginia white-tailed deer, a relatively small race of deer.

Studies on the first red wolves released in the wild have yielded other information, some of which was unexpected. Researchers were somewhat surprised to discover that red wolves are quite social. Most had expected them to hunt individually or in pairs, because that's the pattern for both coyotes and gray wolves that prey on small animals. But two-year-old and yearling red wolves frequently

behave like young gray wolves, remaining with their parents to hunt, defend territory, and help rear the new pups. The first red wolves to be reintroduced are defending territories of 20 to over 100 square miles. Red wolves are often described as more furtive and nocturnal than gray wolves.

THE DRIFT TOWARD EXTINCTION

These shy little wolves suffered the fate of wolves everywhere when European settlers arrived and began remaking the face of the land. Settlers razed forest habitat and put the land to other uses. When unregulated hunting caused deer populations to slump, wolves began preying on sheep and cattle. People retaliated. Wolves were shot, trapped, and poisoned until, in 1980, the species was declared extinct in the wild.

In the late 1960s, the red wolf was making its last stand in 1,700 square miles of sodden marshlands in the shadow of giant petrochemical facilities along coastal Texas and Louisiana. This was miserable wolf habitat. Wolves died from mange, hookworm, and heartworm. Mosquito populations were so high that calves in the area sometimes smothered from all the insects packed in their nostrils.

Things already seemed hopeless for the species when Texas biology professor Howard McCarley began calling attention to another threat: The last red wolves on earth were hybridizing with coyotes. As wolves were eliminated from the western portion of their historic range, coyotes expanded their range eastward. Red wolf populations ultimately dropped so low that wolves began mating with coyotes, leading to what biologists call "hybrid swarm," the loss of species integrity through hybridization. The world's population of red wolves at this point was estimated at 100 beleaguered animals.

Even before there was a federal program to restore endangered species, biologists had begun listing the mammals they considered most at risk of extinction. The red wolf first appeared on that list in 1965. In spite of the listing, a federal predator control program continued to underwrite efforts to eradicate red wolves for another year.

When Congress passed the Endangered Species Act (ESA) of 1973, the red wolf was one of the first species listed. The FWS had already established a red wolf recovery program. It aimed to save red wolves in the wild by isolating the remaining wolves from coyotes. Trappers tried to

By the time scientists became interested in the red wolf, it was too late to begin field studies.

maintain a coyote-free "buffer zone" around the last bit of wolf habitat.

The plan did not work. Federal trappers kept catching animals that they could not positively identify as true wolves or coyote-wolf hybrids. Because hybrids were such a threat to the remaining wolves, animals suspected of having coyote blood were destroyed. It was a gut-wrenching task, because managers were killing animals that looked very much like red wolves at a time when the red wolf was the most endangered wolf in the world. The pain was all the greater because scientists in the program held different views concerning how to determine which animals should be destroyed and which protected.

Managers finally concluded that they had no chance of making the buffer zone program work. Wolves were hybridizing themselves toward extinction, in spite of all the efforts to keep wolves and coyotes separated. The indecision and inadequate support from Washington led some managers in the red wolf program to conclude that there wasn't much will at higher levels of the FWS to restore this unpopular predator.

Ultimately, managers were forced to remove red wolves from the wild in a last-ditch effort to save the species

as zoo animals. That seemed to defy the ESA, which specifically charged the FWS with saving this endangered species in the wild. Even the managers who counseled this course wondered if they were making a terrible mistake. Said one: "We weren't sure we wouldn't be blamed for the extermination of the red wolf." Placing the last red wolves in cages to preserve them seemed perilously close to a notorious rationale from the Vietnam War: "We had to destroy the village in order to save it."

But there was no better option. Federal trappers collected over 400 wild canids, examined them, and sent those that looked like wolves—just 43—to a new captive breeding program run by the Point Defiance Zoo in Tacoma, Washington. Point Defiance was a progressive zoo with a strong interest in preserving endangered animals at a time when such a commitment was uncommon.

Things did not go well at first. After they arrived in Washington, some of the wolves succumbed to diseases. Several more were destroyed, because researchers suspected they carried coyote blood. At one point, the world's population of red wolves stood at 17 animals—and they weren't breeding. Some of the few successful breeders turned out to be

Managers placed red wolves in cages in order to save the animal from extinction.

hybrids. They and their offspring had to be destroyed.

Then, finally, the captive wolves began breeding. They apparently just needed time to adjust to the "concentration camp" atmosphere of life in cages. By 1992, the offspring of those 14 original animals numbered over 200 red wolves.

RESTORATION

When it became clear that the captive breeding program had saved the red wolf from genetic extinction, managers turned their attention to the next challenge. It was time to consider how and where a few wolves could be reintroduced to the wild. Managers faced two very different problems—one political and one biological. They weren't sure what set of techniques—which technology— would allow zoo-reared animals to adjust to life in the wild. And they knew the whole program was likely to encounter political resistance.

Once again, early efforts were discouraging. A release planned for the Land Between the Lakes region of west Kentucky and Tennessee was dropped. The plan was firmly opposed by livestock and hunting groups, and it even drew criticism from environmental groups. Managers later concluded that bungled public relations had doomed the chances of winning public support for the program. While they were disappointed,

managers drew valuable lessons from the experience.

To reduce public opposition, managers decided to take advantage of a 1982 amendment to the ESA. It created an option called the "experimental and non-essential" designation. This special designation allowed managers to conduct a species reintroduction without adhering to all the requirements of the original ESA. For example, experimental and non-essential animals could be removed from the wild if they proved troublesome, an action that was not possible under the original ESA. The designation also allowed managers to permit hunting in the release area, even if it might occasionally result in the death of a wolf.

The experimental and non-essential loophole was something of a two-edged sword, offering some advantages but carrying definite risks. The new designation was likely to reduce public antagonism to the red wolf restoration program. Local people had opposed the Land Between the Lakes release in part because they dreaded the irksome land-use restrictions that would have been imposed by the ESA. For example, if local hunters were barred from using land they had hunted for decades, managers knew the red wolf program

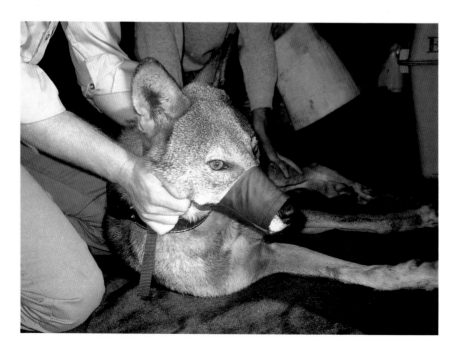

would be highly unpopular. The experimental and non-essential designation offered a way to minimize that sort of trouble.

On the other hand, environmental groups worried that the option was an unwise evasion of important protections built into the ESA. And if any animal needed protection, the red wolf did. With so few of the wolves left on earth, it was a creative fib to call any of them "non-essential" to the breeding program. Still, managers felt the new designation could reduce their political problems.

But where could the wolves be released? In 1984, an insurance company donated to the FWS a parcel of swampy land on the coast of North Carolina. By happy coincidence, the new Alligator River National Wildlife Refuge seemed almost ideal for red wolf reintroduction. The area was large enough, and it contained enough small mammals to support several wolf families. It was sparsely populated by humans. Best of all, the land had no livestock and no coyotes. Because the new refuge was a thumb of land surrounded by water on three sides, managers hoped they could prevent wolves from wandering into areas where they would conflict with humans.

Spokesmen for the red wolf recovery program assured local residents that a new "capture collar" would allow them to keep wolves where they belonged. This collar was a sophisticated refinement of the old radio tracking collar. If it worked the way it was supposed to, the capture collar would give managers an unprecedented degree of control over a free-ranging predator. Using a portable computer, managers could contact a chip in the collar. The chip contains data about the wolf's location and recent activities, data that can be "down-loaded" into the portable computer.

But the most innovative feature of the new collar was its capture function. The collar carries two capsules, either of which can be triggered remotely to inject the wolf with an immobilizing drug. Thus, any wolf that wandered off the refuge could be located, knocked out, and whisked back to the refuge with no stress to the animal and no messy public relations problems.

Although the capture collar helped federal managers sell the red wolf program to the public, complications in its development delayed the first wolf release. The collar's inconsistent performance would continue to plague managers as the restoration program proceeded.

At left, Fish and Wildlife Service managers process a red wolf.

THE TWO TESTS

The red wolf reintroduction program was founded on a rather optimistic supposition: that a wolf reared in a zoo could learn to become a predator capable of killing its own food and withstanding all the threats of life in the wild. The first wolves to be released would be much like a family of humans crawling out of a bomb shelter after a nuclear holocaust. They would have no social support. They would know nothing about the world around them. They would know nothing about finding and killing food.

A moment of hope: Red wolves (above) are released into the wild.

More than most animals, wolves rely on socially acquired knowledge to meet life's challenges. But the reintroduced wolves would have no relevant social learning; in fact, anything they had learned in their zoo years would be hazardous to them in the wild. If they were to survive in a natural environment, the wolves would have to do it on the strength of old instincts and an ability to learn quickly.

Managers were equally concerned about how well humans would tolerate the presence of wolves. It simply would not be possible for managers to protect the wolves from a hostile citizenry. There were too many people walking around with guns during hunting season and too many old logging roads on the refuge for managers to patrol them all. If enough local people decided that red wolves were a threat, the wolves were doomed.

Red wolves were released into the new Alligator River Refuge in 1987, using the "soft release" technique. This was simply a commonsensical protocol based on gradual rather than abrupt release. Wolf families were confined in "acclimation pens," where they could live in safety long enough to identify the local area as their home. Managers minimized contact with humans and even treat-

ed the wolves brusquely to discourage them from developing dog-like bonds with humans.

The wolves were gradually weaned from artificial food. The penned wolves, originally fed dog food, were switched to a diet of fresh carrion (primarily road-killed animals). Wolves were even given live prey, so they could practice killing their own food.

Finally, the doors to the acclimation pens were opened, and red wolves were once again free to roam within at least a limited part of the Southeast. Even after this historic moment, managers occasionally left road-killed deer near the pens, so the transition from dependency to independence would not be too harsh.

Between 1987 and 1992, 36 captive-born red wolves were released in the Alligator National Refuge. Twenty-one died, many killed by vehicles. Some drowned in the swampy refuge, which turned out to be less suitable for wolves biologically than it was politically. Several wolves were killed by other red wolves. In one surprising incident, a female wolf killed her two-year-old daughter when the youngster challenged her right to breed with her mate. Seven of the liberated wolves were later pulled back into the captive breeding program, usually because they persisted in straying. Two simply disappeared. Just six of the 36 zoo-born wolves remain alive and wild at the last accounting.

Though those numbers might seem discouraging, managers consider the program a major success. So far, only one wolf has been killed by a human (the wolf was on the man's property, and the man felt his family was threatened). Best of all, the second and third generation wild-born offspring have done well. Most of the red wolves now living in the refuge have never known life in a cage. The wolves have created family structures. Adult wolves are teaching youngsters how to live as a wolf, just as wolves have done for eons. A genuine population of wild red wolves, small though it may be, is living successfully and naturally on the refuge.

CADES COVE

A second reintroduction took place in 1991, in the southern Appalachians. Four wolves were released in the Cades Cove area of the Great Smoky Mountains National Park. The park is the largest federally owned area in the Southeast that is considered capable of supporting wolves.

One of the most interesting aspects of the second release is that it is an intentional test of two major risks. For one, coyotes are common in the area, and could breed with the wolves if social barriers fail to enforce species integrity. Worse, the release site is in the middle of a large livestock operation. Managers were bold enough to select a "worst-case scenario" site for this release. "If the wolves don't get into trouble here, they won't be a problem anywhere," says Gary Henry.

The second release has generally gone well. Encounters between wolves and coyotes have resulted in aggressive chases, not wolf-coyote hybrids. The wolves have mostly ignored the cattle. "It looks like there's about two days after a calf is born when a coyote or wolf might take it, but when the calves have been on their feet for a day or two, we're okay," says Henry.

Unless new problems crop up, more wolves will gradually be introduced in the Smokies. Additional releases might also be made in the Pocosin Lakes Refuge area west of the Alligator River Refuge. Pocosin Lakes has been called an ideal site for a red wolf release.

THE FUTURE

Public antagonism could still cause problems for the red wolf program.

An agricultural group that was initially neutral has announced its opposition to the program. The change seems due to pressure from western livestock interests trying to prevent the return of wolves to the West.

It seems inevitable that a wolf will kill a dog or a calf from time to time. Then the fragile truce between man and wolf will be tested. On the other hand, public relations for the program have gone well. Many of the road-killed animals fed to wolves during acclimation have been supplied by local citizens who are in favor of red wolf restoration.

The researchers and managers who have guided the red wolf program have come a long way, traveling for the most part without a map. Many challenges must be met before the program meets its ultimate goal of 330 wolves in captivity and 220 in the wild. But the program appears to be headed for a happy conclusion.

The red wolf program tested two great questions whose answers were very much in doubt. The first was whether zoo-reared wolves would be too compromised by their artificial background to succeed in the wild. The second was whether humans could tolerate the close presence of red wolves. It would be impossible to say which challenge was greater: The radical attitudinal change being asked of people or the shock of liberation being experienced by the wolves.

So far, both people and wolves have performed better than just about anybody thought they could. The dramatic comeback of the red wolf, which transformed the species from a few extremely endangered animals in cages to successful, free-roaming predators, is a major triumph of wildlife management.

CHAPTER 9

The Eastern Timber Wolf

According to John Adams, colonists who arrived in New England to begin new lives found that "the whole continent was one continued dismal wilderness, the haunt of wolves and bears and more savage men." The wolves to which Adams referred were eastern timber wolves, *Canis lupus lycaon*. Timber wolves once ranged from southern Ontario to northern Florida, and from the Atlantic seaboard to the Minnesota prairies. Their range essentially coincided with the original hardwood and coniferous forests of the Northeast and Midwest.

Timber wolves are average-sized wolves, weighing from 50 to 100 pounds. Most are gray, although some have cream-colored or black pelage. Since they prey mainly on deer, packs tend to be small, with most containing four to six wolves. Larger packs prevail in places where moose are the main prey.

Timber wolves were trapped and hunted into oblivion as the wave of human settlement rolled westward from the New England shores. In many areas, forests were razed and replaced by towns, factories, and farms. As wolf habitat, these places were lost forever. Things went a bit differently in several midwestern states bordering Canada. When their great white pine forests were logged off, they were replaced by young, second-growth forests in which deer populations boomed and wolves survived in spite of persecution.

Wolf eradication never became the all-out war in Minnesota, Wisconsin, and Michigan that it did elsewhere. In the West, the livestock industry was extremely powerful and totally committed to wolf eradication. By contrast, the upper midwestern states had mixed economies. Wolves were considered a threat to farm livestock and wildlife, but the mining, recreation, and forestry industries had no reason to persecute them. The Great Lakes states never produced notorious "outlaw" wolves with romantic

---

The New World encountered by colonists was "the haunt of wolves and bears."

Original Range of the Eastern Timber Wolf

names. Those states had wolves aplenty, but they lacked the economic and social environment needed to elevate a few wolves to the status of public enemies. It has probably been easier to foster tolerance for wolves in the Upper Midwest, because wolves were not so thoroughly vilified in the region.

Even so, wolves were bountied and killed routinely in the Great Lakes states. Farmers living in the northern regions pressed for wolf control in order to reduce depredation of their

Wolf eradication never became an all-out war in the Great Lakes states.

livestock. Some people killed wolves out of a vague, unexamined sense that wolves were undesirable, and wolves were often killed as a form of moose and deer management. I once asked a retired wolf trapper who had worked for the state of Minnesota if he hated wolves. His denial was indignant: "I was never set against wolves! It was just that they eat so many moose and deer. Our thinking was, 'We are in the business of producing deer, not wolves or something that people don't utilize.'"

Timber wolf numbers dropped steadily under the combined pressures of commercial fur trapping, state and federal predator control programs, and state bounty programs. As more logging roads and fire lanes were cut into the woods, trappers took advantage of the improved access to wolf country. In Minnesota in the 1950s, wolves were shot from airplanes by state agents who hoped to increase deer and moose populations . . . animals that "people could utilize."

By 1965, wolves had been extirpated from 97 percent of their original range in the lower 48 states. All the

Wolves have long been trapped for their hides, and destroyed as a means of managing moose and deer populations.

remaining timber wolves were located in extreme northeastern Minnesota, where managers estimated that between 400 and 800 wolves still lived. A few more lived on Isle Royale, an island in Lake Superior located just off the Minnesota-Ontario border.

The eastern timber wolf received full Endangered Species protection within the lower 48 states in 1974. The federal government—in the form of the U.S. Fish and Wildlife Service (FWS)—assumed management control over gray wolves in all states except Alaska.

MINNESOTA

During the last year in which Minnesota bountied wolves, anyone killing one was considered a local hero and was given a reward of $50. Ten years later, anyone convicted of killing a wolf was likely to receive a stiff fine and might serve time in jail.

That abrupt change created a gap between federal law and local values, a gap felt with special resentment "up north" in wolf country. By unhappy coincidence, at about the time wolves received federal protection, Congress also voted to ban motors in the Boundary Waters Canoe Area Wilderness. The vote was viewed by many residents of northern Minnesota as an unwarranted federal intrusion that threatened the local economy. The two issues merged in the minds of some Minnesotans living in wolf country.

It has always been the fate of the wolf to become someone's symbol. In the early years of federal protection, Minnesota wolves became the symbol of invidious federal meddling in local affairs. Some people expressed their political discontent by killing wolves and defiantly hanging the carcasses on barbed-wire fences.

Special circumstances allowed wolves to persist in Minnesota after they had been extirpated elsewhere. Virtually all of the northeastern corner of the state is wilderness or near-wilderness national forest. The human population is small, and there are no livestock operations in the area. Moreover, Minnesota and Ontario share several hundred miles of border. Much of the terrain on both sides of that border is wild and unsettled. As wolves were killed in Minnesota, empty habitat was filled by fresh recruits dispersing out of Ontario.

Sound wolf management depends on prudent ungulate management. Because of overhunting and several successive harsh winters, the Minnesota deer herd was in desperate

Minnesota Proposed Wolf Management Zones

ESTIMATED ZONE SIZES
(Square Miles)

- Zone 1 - 4,309
- Zone 2 - 1,992
- Zone 3 - 4,554
- Zone 4 - 19,131
- Zone 5 - 55,345

Minneapolis

shape in the early 1970s. In 1971, Minnesota's Department of Natural Resources (DNR) took the drastic step of canceling the whole deer season. The department then developed a new and more sophisticated deer management program. The herd began to build, slowly at first, then more rapidly. By the late 1980s and early 1990s, Minnesota hunters were posting record deer harvests year after year.

The dramatic enlargement of the deer herd helped wolves in two ways. Deer abundance provided the food wolves needed to rear more young wolves and build their own population. At the same time, the anti-wolf spokesmen who had predicted that the resurgent wolf population would "decimate" the deer herd lost all credibility. It was obviously possible to have both deer and wolves. Indeed, by 1992, many managers believed

In the map above, Zones 1, 2, and 3 contain the best wolf habitat.

that Minnesota had more wolves and more deer than was desirable.

THE RECOVERY PLAN

Putting an animal on the endangered species list triggers a chain of events. One of the first steps is the FWS-supervised creation of a "recovery plan" for restoring that species to health. A special team, which included Dave Mech, created an eastern timber wolf recovery plan in 1978. The plan was revised somewhat in 1992.

The team's first priority was to build the strength of wolf populations in Minnesota. Fortunately, there was a simple way to do that. Because a viable if small population existed, the team didn't need to arrange for expensive and complicated wolf transplants. The wolves would naturally build up their own numbers if they simply received protection from humans.

The revised recovery plan established four management zones, each with its own wolf population goal. A variety of management programs encourage strong wolf populations in Zones 1, 2, and 3, the zones containing the best wolf habitat. Zone 4 is marginal wolf habitat. It includes a number of farms situated in brushy land used by wolves, which means

that Zone 4 is the kind of place where a certain amount of livestock depredation is inevitable. Two-thirds of the state, Zone 5, is so highly developed that wolves can't live there without frequently conflicting with humans. Altogether, the team felt that slightly over a third of the state (roughly the northeastern third) qualified as appropriate wolf habitat.

The function of an endangered species recovery plan is to eliminate the need for its own existence. If effective, a recovery plan restores the endangered animal to viability. That animal is "delisted" (dropped from the endangered species list), then the recovery plan is scuttled and replaced by more conventional wildlife management.

In the case of the eastern timber wolf, three criteria must be met before the wolf is delisted. First, the Minnesota population must number between 1,251 and 1,400 animals. Second, a viable secondary population of at least 100 wolves must be created outside of Minnesota (not counting Isle Royale). This population will consist of the combined populations of Wisconsin and Michigan. And finally, those two wolf populations must stabilize at their targeted levels for five successive years. When those three conditions have been satisfied, the eastern timber wolf will be considered fully recovered.

Initially, wolves enjoyed total protection. Nobody could legally kill a wolf, although some people shot or trapped them illegally. In 1978, the U.S. Fish and Wildlife Service downgraded the wolf's status from endangered to "threatened" in Minnesota (but not in Wisconsin and Michigan). That change allowed authorized agents to kill Minnesota wolves that were responsible for killing livestock or pets in some zones.

Minnesota's recovery plan has been a remarkable success. Legal protection and a new public tolerance have allowed Minnesota's wolves to increase their numbers at a fairly steady rate of about three percent per year. That rate of growth is well below the increase of which wolves are capable, which suggests that poaching continues. But a significant amount of wolf mortality is now caused by territorial disputes between wolves, which might be one indication of a recovered population.

By 1989 the Minnesota wolf population stood somewhere between

1,550 and 1,750 animals. In other words, it exceeded its population goal by several hundred wolves. That's great news for fans of wolves . . . but not necessarily for farmers who raise livestock in Zone 4.

THE DEPREDATION PROGRAM

Managers knew they could not restore the wolf without public acceptance. Public acceptance, in turn, required a program dealing with wolves that attack livestock or pets. Minnesota's Animal Damage Control (ADC) program is managed by the U.S. Department of Agriculture, although compensation for damage is provided by the state. Though wolf advocates sometimes resent ADC agents—after all, they are wolf killers—the agents see themselves as a critical element in the overall effort to restore wolves in Minnesota.

When a landowner complains about wolf depredation, an ADC agent seeks evidence to confirm that a wolf was responsible. Some farmers are quick to "cry wolf." Since they receive no compensation for losses due to coyotes or storms, they have an incentive to blame wolves when a calf is missing. If the agent confirms wolf involvement, the offending wolf is trapped, and the landowner

receives compensation. Some 40 cases of wolf depredation are confirmed each year. Annual ADC payments have averaged about $27,000 in recent years.

Depredation reports make interesting reading. The animals attacked include cats and dogs, geese, pigs, horses, sheep, cattle, and turkeys. ADC agents did not confirm the claim in 1991 that wolves attacked two llamas. A single turkey farmer lost 986 birds in 1991, accounting for most of the turkeys lost in the state that year. Wolves sometimes run amok in turkey flocks or herds of sheep, and just one or two such incidents can run up the annual count. Wolves mostly ignore livestock. But on a few farms with special problems, wolf depredation can mean the difference between profit and loss.

ADC agents would rather prevent depredation than deal with its consequences, so part of their work is educational. Depredation is often caused by sloppy animal husbandry. If a farmer fails to dispose of cattle carcasses properly, wolves may discover the carrion and acquire a taste for beef. Similarly, it is foolish for farmers in wolf range to allow cattle to drop their calves in isolated, brushy pastures.

Landowners criticize the ADC program on three counts. They're frustrated when they lose an animal that can't be confirmed as a wolf kill despite circumstantial evidence. Compensation payments are capped at $400 per animal, which is generally $100 to $600 below true market value of adult cattle. Some urban legislators dislike voting for wolf depredation compensation because their constituents are "pro-wolf" or are simply unaware of the depredation problem. People living far from wolf country don't understand how failing to fund

ADC compensation is "anti-wolf" because it drives angry landowners to initiate their own wolf control.

A friend once attended a public hearing on wolf depredation. A farmer whose land included a major wolf travelway had suffered heavy cattle losses. He was accused of lying by a suburban woman who opposed trapping wolves. Her interpretation of Mech's research convinced her that a single pack could not eat as much beef as the farmer claimed he lost. The farmer spluttered in rage and

Failing to fund or create depredation programs may be "anti-wolf," because it drives landowners to initiate their own wolf control measures.

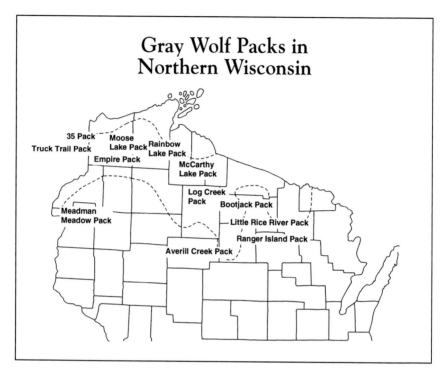

Gray Wolf Packs in Northern Wisconsin

bewilderment. He had been burying cattle ripped apart by wolves, so there was nothing theoretical about the problem as far as he was concerned. Misunderstandings like this can fuel wolf hatred and motivate farmers to defend their property by what they feel is the only means left to them.

Despite its limitations, the ADC program is generally popular with landowners. They appreciate official acknowledgment of their losses, and they would rather receive some compensation than none. Western livestock spokesmen sometimes point to the Minnesota program as an example of the false promise of depredation compensation programs. Objective observers consider it an imperfect program that works fairly well.

The most important statistic coming from the Minnesota ADC program might be the number of livestock that wolves do not kill. About 232,000 cattle and 16,000 sheep live in Minnesota wolf range. According to one analysis, wolves kill about one cow out of every 2,000, and one sheep out of every 1,000 living in their range. Clearly, wild prey is the wolf's preferred food.

WISCONSIN

Bounties were repealed in Wisconsin in 1957 because, as a conservation department official noted, "Posterity wouldn't treat us too well if the last wolf in Wisconsin was killed with a price on its head." As it was, the last wolf was killed a year or two later anyway. The timber wolf was considered extinct in Wisconsin by 1960.

The logical way to restore wolves in Wisconsin was to let them disperse into the state from the expanding Minnesota population. Fortunately, there was a good path available to them. The border country just south of Duluth and Superior is brushy and lightly populated. The only significant barrier to wolf movement in the area is Interstate 35, with its fences and deadly traffic. Otherwise, the country south of the Twin Ports makes a good migration corridor.

And wolves are traveling that corridor. By the winter of 1991-92,

Adrian Wydeven, Wisconsin's wolf researcher, could document 50 adult wolves living in at least 13 packs within the state. Population growth has been steady but slow over the past dozen years. The population has doubled in that time—an annual increase of about eight percent.

But wolves have the biological potential to double their numbers each year. What explains the slow growth? Managers are not entirely sure, but they believe that canine parvovirus has prevented Wisconsin's wolves from raising healthy pups. The problem first came to biologists' attention in the winter of 1982.

Unfortunately, parvo is not the whole problem. Wisconsin's wolves must contend with distemper, Lyme disease, heartworm, and mange—all potentially fatal afflictions. Wolves are extremely hardy animals capable of shaking off diseases that would kill unvaccinated dogs. But the wolves of the Upper Midwest might be encountering more new canine diseases than they can handle in such a short time span. To help them survive this risky period, Wisconsin managers may decide to vaccinate any wolves they're able to trap.

Yet Wisconsin's wolves might be adjusting to parvo. According to the latest count, eight packs are raising pups. The federal timber wolf recovery team set Wisconsin's population goal at 80 wolves. If the wolves have developed some resistance to parvo, they could reach that goal by 1996.

People continue to kill wolves from time to time, but not as frequently as they once did. Humans killed eight of the first ten Wisconsin wolves whose deaths are documented, but only three of the most recent ten. A Wisconsin wolf now has a good chance of dying of natural causes. One radio-collared wolf named "Whistler" lived to an estimated age of between 10 and 12 years. Very few wolves survive so long in the wild. Whistler died in his sleep, possibly a victim of Lyme disease.

In Wisconsin, and elsewhere in the Great Lakes region, wolf managers are concerned about road and highway development. Roads threaten wolves in two ways. Wolves like to travel roads and trails, which makes them vulnerable to being struck by moving vehicles. Roads also open wolf territory to humans, increasing the risk of poaching. Research has identified the critical threshold for wolves as one linear mile of road per square mile of habitat. At or below that level of road development, wolves can maintain their numbers. Above it, they cannot. Anyone armed with that fact and a map can guess where wolves live in northern Wisconsin. For example, one of the largest blocks of roadless land is a swampy area west of Solon Springs, and that region is inhabited by two wolf packs.

Managers are working with highway planners to minimize the impact of roads. For example, Wisconsin 53 is being upgraded from a two-lane to a four-lane highway. In the future, vacationers traveling 53 may notice an unusual amount of brush in the median strip. They're unlikely to guess that the brush was planted to help wolves cross the highway safely by offering a brushy refuge in the middle of the road.

The impact of wolves on the deer herd has always been controversial among many hunters in the Great Lakes states. An adult timber wolf eats the equivalent of a deer every 18 days. Thus Wisconsin's population of 50 adult wolves consumes about 1,000 deer a year, some of which might be carrion. Hunters take about 200,000 deer each year, so humans kill 200 deer for every one taken by wolves. Automobiles kill almost 30 deer for every one killed by wolves. The Wisconsin deer herd is robust at the moment, but if it declines, wolves will not be to blame. When considering the possibility of a drop in deer

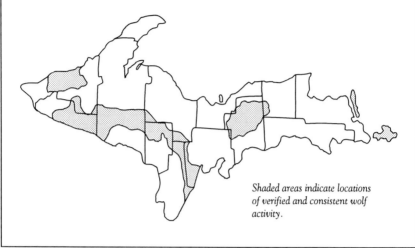

Wolf Areas in Michigan's Upper Peninsula

Shaded areas indicate locations of verified and consistent wolf activity.

numbers, perhaps managers should develop ways to trap cars and release them in other states.

Wisconsin's wolf program owes much of its success to good planning and public relations. Early planning emphasized public involvement. During three years of public hearings, managers practiced "conflict resolution" techniques. According to former wolf manager Dick Thiel, "Frankly, it was hard for us to convince people that we were going to listen to them." People opposed to wolves kept assuming that managers "had a plan in their pocket," and were only going through the motions of seeking public input. Eventually, those participating in the debate realized that their involvement was meaningful.

Managers knew the plan that ultimately emerged from the process would seem less than perfect to almost everybody. Their goal was to end up with a plan everyone could nonetheless accept. Thiel is convinced that the years of public meetings were time well-spent. "If wolves are going to exist anywhere in this world, it will only be with the tolerance of the public. It doesn't matter who you are or how many facts you have on your side. If the public is riled up against you, your plans won't work."

MICHIGAN

When the bounty on Michigan wolves was repealed in 1959, a few wolves still lived in the state's Upper Peninsula. But they didn't last long. The last Michigan wolf was shot or killed by a vehicle in the early 1960s.

During the ensuing years, the timber wolf was like a ghost. It repeatedly made brief, shadowy appearances that could never be confirmed. Managers kept hoping that all the rumored sightings meant a few real wolves were returning to the state. Finally, in 1968, a carcass from the eastern U.P. was positively identified as a wolf. Authenticated wolf sightings have increased dramatically since then.

Michigan's wolf manager, Jim Hammill, has developed a set of clues he uses in distinguishing real sightings from bogus wolf reports:

With a real wolf sighting, people often say they thought they were seeing a deer at first. Then they'll say, "Then I saw that big, brushy tail." If they get close, they'll mention "those huge feet." Then they might say, "But maybe it wasn't a wolf because it just stood there and stared at me." That's when I really start thinking wolf. Feral dogs or coyotes run away as fast as possible. Wolves try to maintain some kind of dignity.

A major breakthrough came in the spring of 1991, when Hammill confirmed the presence of a denning pack—the first wolves to den in Michigan in about three decades. That breeding pair eventually produced a litter of three black and three tawny wolf pups. As many as three packs may have had litters that spring. Previously, most sightings had involved single animals.

Until this breeding occurred, all of Michigan's wolves were dispersers coming from Wisconsin or all the way from Minnesota. A few wolves have entered the U.P. from Ontario, but there are no attractive travel corridors connecting Michigan with the province, so few Michigan wolves have come from Canada.

The conservative, documented count in Michigan now stands at 20 adult wolves. The recovery team's population goal of 30 wolves may be met at almost any time. Legal protection of wolves helped bring the restoration about, but the gains are mostly due to more favorable public attitudes toward wolves.

ISLE ROYALE

Isle Royale is a beautiful, 45-mile-long island that is managed as a wilderness-style national park. The island lies just off the northeastern tip of Minnesota. Isle Royale used to be caribou country, with no resident wolves or moose. Wolves occasionally visited the island, making the 14-mile trek from land to the island when the lake froze in winter. But they did not stay.

Then a series of ecological changes caused the caribou to disappear. Moose swam to the island in the late 1920s and flourished. With no predators to restrain their populations, the moose suffered an erratic boom-bust cycle for many years. In the winter of 1949, another ice bridge connected the island to the mainland, allowing a wolf pack to migrate. This time, the wolves did not leave the island.

Isle Royale's wolf-moose system is the most thoroughly studied predator-prey relationship in the world. In 1958, Purdue's Durward Allen began a study that continues to this day. Many of the most prominent wolf researchers earned their spurs on Isle Royale as graduate students working for Allen.

Island wolves ignore the little airplanes that buzz overhead so much of the time. The dynamics of wolves on the hunt are difficult to study, since the animals move so far so rapidly. But particularly in winter, researchers flying over Isle Royale have learned a great deal about how wolves hunt and how moose defend themselves.

Wolf and moose numbers have soared and dipped in complex patterns over the years. Moose populations have ranged from a low of 200 to the current near-record of 1,600. Wolf numbers have been as high as 50, but now stand at only 12 animals. Isle Royale's famous wolf population is currently in serious trouble. The wolves have not been succeeded at raising a healthy pup for several years, and nobody knows why.

The problem could be due to a food shortage. Although the moose population is extremely large, most of those animals are in the prime of life, and thus are difficult for wolves to kill. Disease, particularly canine parvovirus, might account for the high wolf pup mortality, but that explanation has not yet been confirmed. Some researchers suspect that the pack is suffering from inbreeding, as all of Isle Royale's wolves are descended from the same original pack.

Despite an abundance of moose (left) as prey, Isle Royale's famous wolf population is in serious trouble.

DELISTING

The recovery team estimates that the eastern timber wolf will be eligible for delisting in 2005. That seems realistic. With Minnesota already well beyond its goal, the team needs only to wait for Wisconsin and Michigan to reach a combined population of 100 wolves. Since the combined population is only 30 short of that goal at this writing, delisting can't be far away.

The most controversial aspect of the recovery plan has involved efforts by the DNR to hasten the delisting of the wolf in Minnesota. Minnesota has argued for years that it, not the FWS, should be managing Minnesota's wolves. DNR wants wolf management in the state to include a sport hunting and trapping season in Zone 4, the large region of marginal wolf habitat in north-central Minnesota.

In 1983, the FWS accepted the state's arguments and agreed to permit some sport trapping and hunting. The agreement upset environmentalists and triggered a lawsuit. Arguing that "it is idiotic to hunt an endangered species," environmental groups took the FWS and DNR to court. What came to be known as the Minnesota Wolf Decision concluded with an injunction against sport seasons on wolves.

The delisting controversy hasn't

The wolf recovery team estimates that the eastern timber wolf will be delisted in 2005.

entirely gone away. The issue is not being debated at the moment, but the debate will resume when the recovery plan achieves its objectives and moves to delist the eastern timber wolf. In a few years, the DNR will be managing Minnesota's wolves again. When that happens, some fans of wolves will surely feel threatened.

Yet wolf management in Minnesota will probably change very little after delisting. The DNR is fully committed to maintaining healthy wolf populations. Minnesota's eagerness to resume control of wolf management arises not from a desire to change wolf management, but from what the DNR considers a matter of principle. The department is convinced that it can and should manage all Minnesota animals, including wolves.

Why would Minnesota want to assume all the headaches and controversies involved, when federal wolf management is so successful?

One reason is that the FWS can't seem to fund timber wolf management at acceptable levels. According to one DNR manager, "It is frustrating. The feds maintain control but have lowered the funding priority so much that there isn't money to manage our wolves. I assume they think this program is going pretty well, and

other programs need the money more." State managers are sure they could devote more resources to wolf management if they had responsibility for the program.

The DNR also insists that a limited sport hunting-trapping season is an acceptable and appropriate technique for controlling wolf populations in Zone 4. The department believes that a wolf season might eliminate some of the conflicts between wolves and people. A model for this proposed plan is the state's black bear season. Bears, once shot on an unregulated basis as "varmints," have done well since they have been managed as a big game species with a limited seasonal take. Minnesota seems committed to the principle of management through a sport season, which is the primary management technique for controlling populations of a wide variety of animals.

But wolves aren't bears. When they talk off the record, some DNR managers admit they aren't convinced that a sport season on wolves would be very effective. Because wolves are so elusive, there is no practical way to hunt them with firearms. So a sport season would be limited to trapping, and trapping would never be as popular as hunting with firearms. Moreover, DNR managers realize that

public opinion might prevent them from running any sort of sport season on wolves. Even after they have been delisted, wolves will probably be seen as persecuted and endangered animals.

Delisting will raise the possibility that the Minnesota legislature might meddle in wolf management. It was the legislature, not the DNR, that insisted on wolf bounties for so many years. But Minnesota's legislature isn't likely to take actions harmful to wolves. Minnesotans simply wouldn't let them. The times have changed.

THE FUTURE

When two viable wolf populations exist in the Great Lakes states, the recovery team will investigate possible reintroduction of eastern timber wolves to other states. There are two regions in Maine and one in northern New York that seem appropriate for wolves. Both areas have little human settlement, few roads, and plenty of food. The big challenge will involve fostering positive public attitudes. It has been a very long time since a wolf howled in New England.

In a few years, almost certainly before the turn of the century, the eastern timber wolf will be dropped from the list of endangered species. That will be a dramatic and significant event. Never before has an unpopular predator like the wolf been saved from extinction and successfully restored to such a large range of habitat.

Although western anti-wolf spokesmen try to shore up their position by pointing to problems with wolf recovery in the Upper Midwest, they have to twist the facts in order to do so. The truth is simply this: Wolf restoration is proceeding very well in Minnesota, Wisconsin, and Michigan.

CHAPTER 10

Wolves in the Rockies

The wolf now recolonizing the West has been known as *Canis lupus irremotus*, the northern Rocky Mountain wolf. Its Latin name has been whimsically translated as "the wolf who keeps showing up." Under a new classification system, it is considered *Canis lupus occidentalis*. Regardless of its name, it is indeed the wolf that keeps showing up in the West.

The northern Rocky Mountain wolf is a standard gray wolf, differing from the eastern timber wolf by being slightly larger and more inclined to black pelage. Its ancestral lineage probably goes back directly to the most recently evolved wolves, which were isolated in central Alaska when much of the North American continent was locked in ice.

THE GREAT CAMPAIGN

Wolf hatred was more virulent in the West than anywhere else. The drive to eliminate wolves was often called a "campaign," and it was consciously likened to military combat. The campaign ultimately involved conventional, chemical, and biological warfare. In 1905, Montana cattlemen forced passage of a bill mandating veterinarians to infect wolves with mange and release them to infect others.

Much of the wolf killing was done with strychnine. According to historian Stanley Young, "There was a sort of unwritten law of the range that no cowman would knowingly pass by a carcass of any kind without inserting in it a goodly dose of strychnine sulfate, in hopes of killing one more wolf." Millions of wolves and coyotes died, plus unintended victims such as badgers, foxes, and hawks. According to writer Barry Lopez, cattlemen also poisoned horses, cattle, dogs, and even a few of their own children. The primary motivation was economic. Ranchers hated wolves on general principle, but especially because they killed cattle and sheep. And some of the cattlemen surely suffered

The drive to eliminate wolves from the West was called a "campaign," and it was likened to military combat.

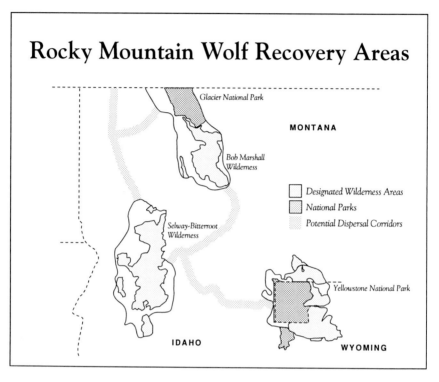

Rocky Mountain Wolf Recovery Areas

Glacier National Park

MONTANA

Bob Marshall
Wilderness

☐ Designated Wilderness Areas
☐ National Parks
▒ Potential Dispersal Corridors

Selway-Bitterroot
Wilderness

Yellowstone National Park

IDAHO

WYOMING

significant losses to wolves.

European settlers dramatically disrupted the ecology of the West. Weak or non-existent game laws led to serious overhunting of elk, deer, and moose. The bison, of course, was extirpated. Vast cattle herds and sheep flocks grazed where wild game once fed. Wolves had the choice of eating livestock or starving.

Some livestock depredation, ironically enough, might have been a by-product of the anti-wolf campaign. The heavy mortality suffered by wolves disrupted their normal social structures and hunting patterns. The disruption made it less likely that the survivors could make an honest living hunting wild prey.

Viable wolf populations disappeared from Montana, Wyoming, and Utah in the 1920s. Intensive predator control programs eliminated wolves from Glacier and Yellowstone parks at about the same time. By the 1930s, the wolf was mostly an unpleasant memory in the West.

THE WOLF THAT KEEPS SHOWING UP

Wolves remained absent from the Rockies for half a century. Now and then, somebody reported seeing an animal that might have been a wolf. These shadowy reports increased sharply in the 1970s, convincing biologists that a few dispersers from Canada were filtering back into the empty habitat. But those lone wolves weren't meeting other wolves and forming packs. And in spite of federal protection as members of an endangered species, they were not surviving for very long.

In the early 1980s, researchers confirmed the existence of a wolf pack in Glacier Park. Those first arrivals must have thought they had dispersed their way into wolf heaven. Glacier held bountiful herds of fat mule deer that were almost totally innocent about predators. Glacier's wolf population began increasing at a rate of 40 percent per year. Four packs now hunt in or near Glacier.

Once established in Glacier, wolves began traveling down the spine of the Rockies with increasing frequency. Today they're showing up in all sorts of places, particularly in western Montana. A pack has denned more or less continuously in Montana's Ninemile Valley since 1990. Biologists have heard what they believed to be howling and found wolf tracks in Wyoming's Shoshone National Forest, just 50 miles southeast of Yellowstone Park.

A separate but similar migration has occurred along the western slope of the Rockies. Wolves moving out of British Columbia are repopulating empty habitat in Washington. State biologists estimate that Washington's wolf population stands at between 15 and 20 animals, but is increasing. Oregon, too, seems to be attracting wolves. State officials continue to doubt that wolves are living permanently in the state, but over 30 sightings of wolf-like animals have been reported in recent years within the Rogue River National Forest and in nearby areas.

Idaho remains an enigma. After many years of isolated sightings, reported sightings became much more frequent in the 1980s. In 1983, one wolf was often seen in the Kelly Creek area of northern Idaho. One collared female has been drifting around the state's northern border,

living alternately in two provinces (British Columbia and Alberta) and two states (Montana and Idaho). A pair of wolves began keeping company in Idaho's Bear Valley in 1991. Biologists were convinced that the wolves were on the verge of starting a pack. Later that year, one was illegally poisoned.

Although wolves have been reported by the public in Idaho for 20 years, biologists have not confirmed a single succcessful breeding. That's especially frustrating because Idaho has more suitable wolf habitat than just about any other state. Moreover, the state's citizens are highly supportive of wolves. The evidence suggests that poaching has been just serious enough to keep wolves from denning and securing a foothold in central Idaho.

Wolves suddenly seem to be materializing throughout the Rockies.

Why do wolves suddenly seem to be popping up all over the Rockies? In the 1950s, Canadian wolf management was as backward as American management had been at the turn of the century. Then wildlife managers in the western provinces adopted more progressive policies. They stopped wolf poisoning in 1961 and began managing wolves as a big game species with regulated seasons. Wolf population densities increased, particularly in the 1980s. Coincidentally, a combination of mild winters and rejuvenated habitat triggered increases in deer and elk populations on the U.S. side of the border. Canadian wolves began moving south.

THE YELLOWSTONE DEBATE

Although wolves are recolonizing several western states, the great public debate on wolf restoration in the West has centered on Yellowstone Park. Perhaps that was inevitable. The wolf is America's most symbolic animal. Yellowstone is America's oldest and most famous national park. The Yellowstone wolf controversy has acquired the status of a watershed resource decision—one of those high-profile political events that marks a major shift in social thinking.

When the wolf was declared endangered in 1973, the Fish & Wildlife Service (FWS) became responsible for preparing restoration plans. A plan materialized quickly in the Great Lakes states, but not in the West. The eastern timber wolf recovery plan had been in operation for several years by the time the FWS issued its plan for wolves in the northern Rockies.

The plan called for wolf restoration in three areas. FWS researchers thought wolves would naturally recolonize northwestern Montana (the Glacier-Bob Marshall region) and central Idaho (the Selway-Bitteroot

As illustrated by the poster above, anti-wolf sentiment remains strong in the West.

area). Both areas offer abundant ungulate populations and extensive areas free of human settlement. Wolf restoration in those areas, the planners thought, could be achieved by recolonization, relying upon the natural mechanism of dispersal. If dispersing wolves could be protected from humans, they would eventually find and use the habitat.

The plan also called for the return of wolves to Yellowstone National Park. Because the park lies several hundred miles from viable Canadian wolf populations, managers believed the best way to restore wolves to

Yellowstone would be to put them there through a technique called "transplanting." Their plan called for trapping wolves in Canada, moving them to Yellowstone, then holding the wolves in habituation pens until the animals could be freed via the "soft release" protocol developed for the red wolf.

Publication of the restoration plan provoked a noisy debate. Pro-wolf and anti-wolf groups went at each other until the fur flew. Several western congressmen distinguished themselves by spouting statements about wolves that were both prejudicial and irresponsible.

A Montana senator predicted that, if wolves returned to the park, "There'll be a dead kid within a year."

An Idaho senator told schoolchildren that wolves "pose a real danger to humans."

A Montana congressman declared that wolves are "like cockroaches in your attic."

At public meetings, cattlemen brandished signs comparing the wolf to Saddam Hussein.

A very different response emerged when pollsters measured national and regional public opinion. Yellowstone visitors favored wolf restoration by a six-to-one ratio. Public opinion polls in Idaho, Montana, and Wyoming showed majority support for returning wolves to the park. In early hearings for an environmental impact statement on restoring wolves to Yellowstone, pro-wolf forces outnumbered wolf opponents almost seven to one. Yet the opposition has remained determined.

Much is at stake. According to an Idaho sheep raiser, "It's not the wolf we're scared of, but the wolf managers and all the rules and regulations they'll bring with them." For many ranchers, the effort to bring back the wolf represents the onset of many disturbing changes that will affect their way of life. An Idaho rancher told a reporter, "The wolf is just the opening wedge for those folks who only see mountains and animals out here, and who don't care about humans who need to make a living." The wolf, ever doomed to be somebody's symbol, has become a symbol of Big Government and the passing of the Old West.

At times, National Park Service officials have supported wolf restoration. At other times, they have deferred to anti-wolf forces. Even so, one of the most forceful statements on behalf of returning wolves to the park came from the service's John Varley. "If we restore wolves to Yellowstone," Varley said, "it will be

the only place left in the 48 states that has all of the native animals and plants that were here when white men hit the shores of North America. Now there are none. Why can't we have just one place like that?"

Major environmental groups have made the Yellowstone wolf restoration a showcase issue, because it is the most crucial test to date of the Endangered Species Act. If wolves can be barred from a place in which they so obviously belong, the ESA will be reduced to a paper tiger. Conversely, if a controversial predator can be restored in such a prominent location, the ESA will be stronger than ever. According to Hank Fischer, northern Rockies representative of Defenders of Wildlife, "If we succeed in restoring wolves to Yellowstone, it will make an important statement about the role of predators in natural ecosystems. It's an action that will be noticed around the world."

The politically powerful wolf opponents probably would have won the Yellowstone debate by now if they had the facts on their side. However, after studying all the relevant scholarship, an expert panel concluded that

Wolves may naturally recolonize Yellowstone National Park.

wolves pose no threats to humans or ungulate populations in the park. The panel's report, *Wolves For Yellowstone?*, found no reason to bar wolf restoration.

TO TRANSPLANT OR NOT TO TRANSPLANT?

One of the most complex issues in the debate is whether wolves should be transplanted or allowed to return on their own. It is an issue that not only splits the two sides (pro-wolf and anti-wolf), but divides the partisans within each camp.

Ranchers confront a dilemma. As much as they hate the idea of transplanting wolves to Yellowstone, the likely alternative—natural recolonization—is even more threatening. If the park is recolonized naturally, wolves in the ecosystem will be a fully protected endangered species, just as the wolves of northwestern Montana now are. That status allows little flexibility in dealing with wolves that might stray out of the park to attack cattle or sheep. According to a spokesman for the Idaho Wool Growers, "The worst thing that could happen is for the wolf to come in on its own and be protected as king of all the animals."

Wolf advocates are also divided. Some prefer to let the wolves recolonize the park unaided, at a time of their own choosing. The prospect is appealing because it would be a natural event. Some wolf advocates are repelled by all the machinery of manipulated restoration: the pens, collars, and computers. Above all, they reason, if wolves recolonized the park, they would enjoy the full protection of the ESA.

Nevertheless, most wolf advocates want wolves reintroduced under the relaxed "experimental and non-essential" ESA standards. For one thing, they fear it will take too long for wolves to recolonize Yellowstone without assistance (40 years, by one estimate). One wolf in the park won't do anything for restoration. Two or three wolves might not find each other. Even one denning pack wouldn't do much to repopulate Yellowstone in the short run.

Moreover, conservationists recognize that the greatest threat to wolf restoration is the entrenched hatred of wolves and the ESA. Ranchers have been managing wolves their own way for a century and a half. Many cattlemen have a rifle mounted in the window of their pickups and would not hesitate to shoot a wolf in defense of their way of life. If ranchers remain implacably opposed to wolves, everyone involved—especially the wolves—will suffer. That's why conservationists want to strike a bargain with western landowners: Let us have wolves in Yellowstone, and we'll let you have the flexibility to control wolves that prey on livestock.

At the request of Congress, a special committee was created in 1991 to hammer out a compromise management program. It included managers, conservationists, hunters, and ranchers. Compromise, however, proved elusive. Pro-wolf members ended up dissenting from the committee's final report because it recommended placing all western wolves (including those in Idaho, Montana, and Wyoming) in the "experimental and non-essential" category. They objected to granting ranchers the right to kill any wolf that the cattlemen felt was "harassing" livestock. In short, the committee's management would have exposed too many wolves to too much arbitrary mortality. Nevertheless, something like this plan—but with more protection for wolves—will probably be implemented.

The plan may not be needed if wolves recolonize the park on their own—an outcome that seems increasingly likely. Wolves are already denning 220 miles from the park boundary. Because dispersers can log 500 miles in search of a new home, the park is well within the range of wolves.

A breeding pack might already be living in Yellowstone. In 1992, a hunter shot a wolf, thinking it was a coyote, just outside the park's southern boundary. It was apparently a black male wolf with a group of four coyotes. Near that site, park rangers have spotted several animals that they thought were wolves. A cinematographer has filmed what looks like a wolf in Yellowstone's Hayden Valley—right in the center of the park. Wolf experts have had a lively disagreement about this animal, but most believe it's a wolf.

This flurry of sightings is similar to what happened near Glacier Park, and it probably portends a similar outcome. Wolves might return to Yellowstone on their own, perhaps while ranchers and wolf advocates are still locked in battle about whether wolves should be transplanted to the park.

BIOLOGICAL ISSUES

If the FWS decides to reintroduce wolves to Yellowstone, how difficult will that prove to be? "It is doable, but probably will not proceed as smoothly as the public expects," according to Steve Fritts, Wolf

Recovery Coordinator for the Northern Rocky Mountains.

For several reasons, restoring red wolves to the Southeast was a more severe challenge. The release technology was totally untested. At first, managers did not keep red wolves in acclimation pens long enough before releasing them. Some wolves died in an effort to find their way back "home." Worse, the red wolves were zoo animals with no knowledge of how to live outside a cage.

Any wolves translocated to Yellowstone will be wild animals live-trapped from Rocky Mountain habitat in Canada. These wolves will not know the bizarre terrain of Yellowstone as the park's original wolves once did, but that will be their principal disadvantage. Since elk are so common in Yellowstone, researchers will probably stock the park with Canadian wolves from packs that know how to hunt elk.

Still, managers like Fritts hope the public understands some translocated wolves will probably die. Fritts points out, "For all the talk about wolf reintroduction, the soft release process has not been tried with wild gray wolves." There could be

Wolves translocated from Canada to Yellowstone would not be familiar with the park's unusual terrain.

surprises. "We will consider various approaches," says Fritts, "but all would involve a lengthy holding period at the release site to break the tendency of wolves to leave that site and return to their former home." Managers will plan for all contingencies, then "expect the unexpected."

DEPREDATION

Once they are established in Yellowstone, will wolves leave the park and prey on livestock? Most wolf advocates believe some wolves are likely to wander out of the park and that a few will prey on cattle and sheep. It is difficult to predict how serious the problem will be, though the research is reassuring. Studies in Minnesota and Alberta show that wolves rarely attack livestock. Western wolf opponents contend that those studies are not relevant because of differences in terrain and livestock husbandry. But wolf advocates respond that the most relevant precedent is the past decade in northwestern Montana, where wolves have lived near cattle without causing significant problems.

Most (but not all) wolf advocates also acknowledge the need for a fair and effective depredation program. A good program would compensate ranchers for livestock losses, and would remove those wolves that acquire the habit of preying on livestock. The program will have to be very good indeed if it is to soften the ranchers' opposition to wolves. The western cattleman is stubborn, fiercely independent, and suspicious of all federal programs except those that provide inexpensive grazing rights on public land.

Managers are discussing use of the capture collar. That collar, first used in the red wolf program, has proven reliable and valuable in research in the Upper Midwest and elsewhere. Under the plan, if a wolf leaves the park and attacks livestock, it would be captured and collared. If that wolf repeats the offense, managers could trigger the collar to drug the wolf, which would allow them to capture the animal without delay. It won't be easy to sell that notion to some wolf advocates, who are aghast at the notion of collars, let alone collars fitted with darts and drugs.

The capture collar has already proven its worth. After the adult wolves of the Ninemile pack killed a steer in the spring of 1992, the pair was captured. Managers decided to give them one last chance, releasing the wolves rather than destroying them or moving them. But before they were released, the female was fitted with a standard beeping radio collar while the male was given one of the new capture collars. That meant managers could instantly capture the pair if they attacked livestock again. Fortunately, they did not. Were it not for the capture collar and the way it enables managers to control wolves, there might not be wolves in the Ninemile today.

One environmental group working for wolves, Defenders of Wildlife, has created its own fund to compensate ranchers for livestock losses. According to Hank Fischer, "Our goal is to shift any economic burden associated with wolf recovery away from individual livestock producers and toward the millions of people around the country who want to see wolves restored." Defenders of Wildlife pays fair market value for livestock lost to wolves, which is more than the state of Minnesota is doing. About $12,000 has been paid out since 1987.

The protracted legal battle over wolf restoration in the West proves that wolf opponents have mastered the delaying tactics often used by environmentalists. There isn't room here to summarize all the legal maneuvering. At long last, the U.S. Congress has grown impatient with all the delays, and has ordered the FWS to prepare an Environmental Impact Statement for wolf recovery in Yellowstone and central Idaho. If all goes well, wolves could be released in the park as early as 1995.

PROSPECTS

One way or another, wolves will return to Yellowstone, and probably very soon. The American public wants wolves in the park, and the majority of local citizens agree. The FWS knows that wolves belong in Yellowstone. The National Park Service wants wolves returned, though it can't always say so in a forthright manner. The nation's foremost environmental groups have made the return of wolves to Yellowstone their highest priority. The ESA requires the restoration of wolves to ideal habitat such as Yellowstone.

All the biological requirements for wolf restoration have been met. The task remaining for managers and wolf advocates is that of establishing the right social environment, so that restoration can proceed as smoothly and humanely as possible.

CHAPTER 11

The Lobo

To appreciate the plight of the lobo, or Mexican wolf, consider these facts. The Mexican wolf exists today only as a few zoo animals. All derive from a perilously narrow genetic base, and all have been separated from life in the wild by one, two, or three generations. Some of these caged wolves will probably be released at isolated sites in the Southwest, where they'll have to learn how to be wild wolves in a very short time and in an unnatural way. Many—perhaps half—will die. And, while Mexican wolf restoration has garnered considerable public support, many people in the Southwest still regard killing wolves as an affirmation of community values.

In short, the lobo is the most endangered wolf in North America, and quite possibly the most endangered wolf in the world.

Both the Fish and Wildlife Service (FWS) and environmental groups have neglected the Mexican wolf in their preoccupation with the Yellowstone wolf controversy. Yet, in spite of old crimes and recent omissions, the lobo exists. It appears to be doing well in captivity, and it may soon flourish in a few sites in the wild.

THE SOLE SURVIVOR

E.A. Goldman, wolfdom's consummate taxonomic splitter, believed there were once five races of wolves inhabiting the Southwest: the Texas wolf, the lobo, the southern Rocky Mountain wolf, and two intergrades. That degree of complexity was almost surely too fussy, but it hardly matters, since four of Goldman's five southwestern wolves are now extinct. We are left with but a single southwestern race of wolf—*Canus lupus baileyi*. Unfortunately, the precise history of the different wolf races is one of many issues that biologists can't properly research, because no objective studies were done before it became too late.

The Mexican wolf is the smallest gray wolf in America, weighing from 50 to 90 pounds. Mexican wolves live further south than any other North

---

The lobo (Mexican wolf) is the most endangered wolf in North America.

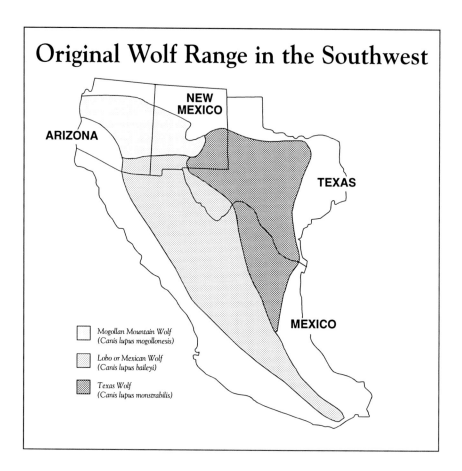

Original Wolf Range in the Southwest

ARIZONA

NEW MEXICO

TEXAS

MEXICO

Mogollan Mountain Wolf
(Canis lupus mogollonesis)

Lobo or Mexican Wolf
(Canis lupus baileyi)

Texas Wolf
(Canis lupus monstrabilis)

American gray wolf. Some observers believe Mexican wolves differ from northern wolves by virtue of shorter and more pointed ears, shorter coats, and a tendency toward ruddy pelage color. Yet the differences should not be exaggerated. The lobo looks like what it is: a small, southern-dwelling race of the gray wolf. It seems likely that the Mexican wolf descended from an early race of North American wolves; thus it is a relatively primitive and coyote-like gray wolf.

A recent genetic analysis of Mexican wolves surprised some researchers. The mitochondrial DNA of Mexican wolves contains a unique pattern, which makes a strong case for considering the Mexican wolf a distinct subspecies of gray wolf. This finding was a major reason that an international council of wolf scientists called the Mexican wolf the "highest priority need for wolf conservation the world over."

HISTORICAL PERSPECTIVES

According to historical accounts, wolves were relatively scarce in the Southwest when European settlers arrived. That only makes sense. Much of the region consists of flat, arid plains that could not support enough ungulates to feed many wolves.

The lobo was primarily an animal of montane forests, those relatively moist and thickly forested watershed regions on the gentle slopes of mountain ranges. The brushy, mid-slope regions were almost the only places in which southwestern wolves could satisfy two of their basic needs: abundant water and large prey animals.

Everything changed when European settlers arrived. White settlers badly overhunted mule deer, elk, and the little Coues white-tailed deer. In their place, settlers filled the plains with cattle and sheep. "By the late 1880s," writes historian David E. Brown, "the Southwest was one large livestock ranch." Brown has suggested that the "large and poorly guarded livestock herds . . . may actually have led to an increase in wolves." Deprived of natural food, wolves took advantage of the abundant bovine protein.

The period that followed was curious. Never, before or since, were so many predator exterminators employed to destroy so few animals in order to produce such dubious benefits. Federal "wolfers" in the Predatory Animal and Rodent Control (PARC) program routinely exaggerated the economic impacts of wolf depredation, and even exaggerated the size of the animals they destroyed. National Park Service officials, eager to win support for the newly formed agency, joined in the great campaign to rid the Southwest of wolves, bears, and mountain lions.

As wolf populations fell, the last survivors became extremely wary. Several southwestern wolves gained notoriety, much like human outlaws. They had names: Las Margaritas, Old One Toe, the Chiricahua Wolf. When one of these famous cattle-killers was destroyed, newspapers trumpeted the news all over the Southwest. The White Lobo, supposedly the last wolf in Texas, was killed for a $500 bounty in 1925. After examining the corpse, the man who shot her decided that the White Lobo's legendary ability to avoid baited traps was due to the fact she had no sense of smell.

The spirit of the times can be sensed in one of Ernest Thompson Seton's classic stories, "The Currumpaw Wolf." As Seton describes him, this lobo had an uncanny knack for eluding the army of humans that pursued him. Seton finally managed to trap the wolf's mate, Blanca. According to the writer, the heartsick Currumpaw wolf then blundered into traps baited with his mate's scent. When Seton staked him down near food and water, the proud lobo stared at the distant hills and died . . . presumably of a broken heart. The story is too melodramatic to be credible, but it is interesting for its odd tone. When Seton wrote, he saw himself as the hero of the piece. His story now strikes most readers as a chilling indictment of warped values.

Despite sensational tales about ghostly, uncatchable individuals, the wolf was not difficult to eradicate. In just 11 industrious years, PARC agents eliminated viable wolf populations throughout the Southwest. The program continued in a "mopping-up" mode for several more decades. Indeed, wolf eradication continued long after it had become morally indefensible, long after people should have known better.

The last wolf killing in the American Southwest had the qualities of a political assassination. In the mid-1970s, a wolf that came to be known as the "Aravaipa wolf" was sighted

Above, a Mexican wolf strolls through simulated natural habitat.

several times in mountains west of Sulphur Springs, Arizona. When the Mexican wolf was placed on the list of endangered species, ranchers feared that the Aravaipa wolf might become the founder of a resurgent wolf population. Arizona stockmen quietly put the word out that they would pay a bounty to anyone who took care of the problem. The Aravaipa wolf became the first wolf to die as a direct consequence of the Endangered Species Act (ESA).

Wolves kept wandering out of Mexico into the U.S. as late as the 1970s. Then, land use changes in Mexico caused lobos below the border to fall under the same persecution that had wiped them out above the border. Unemployed U.S. wolfers moved south and continued their work. A new chemical, Compound 1080, helped eliminate lobos from all or most of Mexico by 1982.

DODGING THE BULLET OF EXTINCTION

The Fish and Wildlife Service (FWS) listed the Mexican wolf as an endangered species in 1976. Unlike the timber wolf, which in the 1970s was endangered in the United States but prolific in Canada, the Mexican wolf was—and is—highly endangered in the genetic sense. It faces extinction, because there is no known, viable wild population anywhere that can be tapped for a recovery program.

In 1977, the FWS hired Roy T. McBride, a famous wolf trapper, to live-trap as many wild lobos as possible. McBride had trapped Las Margaritas, possibly the Southwest's most elusive wolf, and he was as knowledgeable as any man in the ways of Mexican wolves. He eventually caught five lobos in the Durango region of Mexico. Only one was female, but she was pregnant. Ultimately, four wild wolves became the seed stock for the captive breeding program.

In 1990, McBride returned to the Mexican states of Chihuahua and Durango to see if he could find more wild Mexican wolves. He never got a chance to look. Former cattle operations had been replaced by marijuana fields that were guarded with deadly force. Ironically, the marijuana lands might offer the only hope for Mexico's wolves . . . that is, if any still lived when the drug kingpins replaced the cattlemen. Wolves cannot live outside the marijuana plantations, McBride believes, because the rest of Mexico has become too heavily developed.

Some biologists still hope that a few small family groups of Mexican wolves may exist in the Sierra Madre Occidental, a mountain range in northwest Mexico. Salvaging a remnant population is usually less tricky and expensive than reintroducing a zoo-raised population. If someone finds even one or two lobos to add to the gene pool in the captive breeding program, the Mexican wolf's future would be far brighter. But most researchers feel that it is too late.

The bloodlines of the lobos in the captive breeding program might be augmented by contributions from wolves in other zoos. Mexican and U.S. zoos house a number of animals called Mexican wolves. The animals have not yet been certified as authentic lobos, but a new genetic analysis technology might allow scientists to make a positive determination. Unless the zoo animals are verified as pure Mexican wolves, the lobo's future rides on the genes of just four wolves.

The population of authenticated Mexican wolves in the captive breeding program stands at 49. In 1992, "Don Diego" died of cancer at the ripe old age of 15. Don Diego was the last surviving Mexican wolf born in the wild, one of the males trapped by McBride. While he lived, Don Diego sired eight litters of pups.

Why are there so few wolves after a decade and a half of captive breeding? According to Peter Siminski, curator of mammalogy and ornithology at the Arizona-Sonora Desert Museum,

"There was no place to put more wolves, so we didn't want to run the numbers up. There was a lack of interest and a lot of uncertainty about the future of the program. But that's all changed in the past two years."

In other words, the captive breeding program has been treading water for over a decade, simply keeping the lobo alive genetically. Siminski believes big population increases will come "when we get going."

That time is apparently at hand. Ten institutions are currently breeding lobos, and several more have applied to join the program. When the total population of Mexican wolves reaches 100 animals, managers will feel ready to begin wild releases.

DELAY AND RECOVERY

In 1979, the FWS created a Mexican Wolf Recovery Team. The agency produced a recovery plan that was signed by U.S. and Mexican officials in 1982. The team did not have many management options. It could not hope that wolves would naturally recolonize old habitat. The wolves could be restored to the Southwest only if people put them there, using the relaxed regulations of the ESA's "experimental and non-essential" clause.

There were also very few options

when it came to location. Most of the Southwest is too highly developed to accept wolves. The recovery team felt that the most optimistic and attainable goal would be to establish several isolated, viable populations in the Southwest totalling at least 100 wolves. Such an accomplishment would allow the lobo to be downgraded from "endangered" to "threatened" status.

A plan is no good unless someone implements it, and for several years the Mexican wolf recovery program lay dormant. The FWS could have prepared the ground for wolf recovery in the early 1980s by conducting public information and education projects. The service did virtually nothing

because it lacked funding and—according to some critics—because senior officials were reluctant to push an unpopular project.

At one point, the FWS announced that it would not proceed with wolf restoration unless it received full support from state wildlife agencies. That position virtually doomed the recovery program, because the wildlife departments of Arizona, New Mexico, and Texas did not want to promote a program opposed by powerful livestock and sport hunting groups. The FWS position seemed to ignore the ESA, which does not allow state agencies to supersede federal management of endangered species.

Things finally began to move in

1986, when local and national pro-wolf groups pressured the FWS to fulfill its responsibilities under the ESA. The FWS asked the wildlife agencies of the three states to propose possible reintroduction sites. Texas stonewalled, claiming that there was no place in the entire state suitable for wolves. Arizona offered 15 sites, but claimed the sites had not been evaluated. New Mexico said the only place wolves could be restored within its borders was to portions of the White Sands Missile Range, a 4,000-square-mile facility used by the U.S. Army as a bombing practice range.

All attention suddenly turned to White Sands. The range had some suitable habitat, it was isolated from human interference, and—best of all—it had no cattle. Wildlife researchers determined that White Sands could hold as many as 40 wolves. It seemed a likely prospect for the first release.

Identification of White Sands as a potential release site galvanized opposition to the Mexican wolf program. Livestock and hunting groups organized to block wolf restoration in White Sands. In 1987, in the midst of the debate, an Army commander flatly announced, "We do not want wolves on the White Sands Missile Range." The regional FWS director stunned pro-wolf groups by announcing, "The

wolf reintroduction program, as of now, is terminated."

Wolf advocacy groups rebounded. They formed a Mexican Wolf Coalition that sued the departments of Interior and Defense for failing to implement the ESA. The logjam broke. The Army reversed its opposition to wolves on White Sands. Wolf educational materials developed by the FWS but never released were finally put into circulation. Congress appropriated a modest amount of money for Mexican wolf reintroduction. In 1990, the FWS appointed Dave Parsons as the coordinator for the Mexican wolf program.

None of this progress would have been possible without stout advocacy from both national and local wolf groups. The Defenders of Wildlife has begun turning its attention to the lobo. Strong Mexican wolf committees in New Mexico, Arizona, and Texas have raised thousands of dollars and conducted many public information projects. In effect, the private sector is doing the educational work the FWS cannot do because of inadequate staff and funds.

Mexican wolf reintroduction received support from a surprising quarter recently. Both the Arizona Cattle Grower's Association and the Arizona Wool Producers have adopted resolutions favoring wolf reintroduction. The resolutions are highly conditional, but they are remarkable and unprecedented. Never before has the livestock industry shown even lukewarm tolerance for wolves, let alone official support for wolf recovery.

How did this happen? Some wolf supporters believe the Arizona livestock groups don't think the FWS can meet their conditions, which means the resolution will effectively block wolf recovery. Other, less cynical observers say there are some progressive ranchers in Arizona who recognize that the public is unhappy with them for over-grazing public lands. Those ranchers don't want to be on the wrong side of popular opinion in another high-profile controversy.

The simplest explanation is that Arizona's livestock interests assessed the popularity of wolf recovery and made a difficult political decision. Representatives of pro-wolf groups told ranchers they could oppose wolf restoration and be defeated, or they could participate as cooperative partners in a program that would proceed with or without their support.

In addition to New Mexico's White Sands, a site in Texas is being studied for wolf reintroduction. Managers are looking at the 1,200-square-mile Big Bend National Park and the nearby 400-square-mile Big Bend Ranch State Park. Public hunting is not allowed in these parks. About 35 percent of the Big Bend area is considered prime wolf habitat.

PROSPECTS

The Mexican wolf restoration program has come to life at an unpropitious moment. In spite of growing public interest in the lobo, the federal deficit has put severe pressure on funding for all endangered species. In a sorry turn of events, the highly endangered lobo must compete with the highly endangered red wolf (plus the eastern timber wolf and the northern Rocky Mountain wolf) for precious federal funds.

By any assessment, the Mexican wolf project is woefully under-funded. Parsons doesn't have a staff, and must rely on wolf advocacy groups to educate the Southwest concerning what it lost when it eradicated the wolf. "Once you get a program up and running, it's easier to get continued funding," Parsons laments, "but it's hard to get going." That is frustrating because, as Parsons notes, "The Mexican wolf is the most endangered wolf in the country, or even the world. I'm not just trying to extend the range of a wolf that has a viable population in other portions of its range. I'm trying to protect a unique genetic entity that's teetering on the brink of extinction."

Parsons assesses his program's challenges by noting, "We've got all the political issues and problems that the Yellowstone wolf has. We've got the opposition from the livestock industry and sport hunting groups. We have all the concerns about private property rights. What we don't have is many wolves."

Public opinion is moving in the right direction. By some estimates, 65 to 70 percent of the general public supports wolf reintroduction, five to 10 percent don't care, and the rest are adamantly opposed. Public opinion seems most favorable in Arizona and most opposed in Texas.

The Mexican wolf reintroduction program currently faces less bitter opposition than the Yellowstone wolf. This might seem like a ray of hope for the lobo. Yet wolf advocates fear it may simply reflect the fact that their program is too weak to threaten anyone. When the time comes to reintroduce lobos in the Southwest—perhaps in 1995 or 1996—more frenzied opposition may appear.

One of the most vigorous supporters of Mexican wolf reintroduction is Bobbie Holaday, the founder of Preserve Arizona's Wolves (P.A.W.S.). "I would like to think we have more progressive ranchers in the Southwest than in the northern Rockies," Holaday says, "but we won't know until the program gathers strength." Holaday is hopeful: "I know I will never see a wolf in the wild in my lifetime. They're just too wary. But it's my fondest hope that, someday, I will hear one."

At this time, it's too early to predict success for the Mexican wolf restoration program. Nothing about this program is sufficiently abundant. There are too few wolves. The existing wolves draw on a much narrower genetic base than is desirable. The program is badly underfunded. There are few places to put wolves in the Southwest where they can't threaten livestock. The state wildlife agencies, particularly in Texas, have offered too little support. With a few exceptions, the Southwest's senators and congressmen have waltzed around the controversy.

And yet, in spite of everything, the lobo is closer to some limited form of recovery than it has been in decades. The program has been slow to get moving, but it is moving now, and many observers are reasonably confident that it will succeed. Until it does, the Mexican wolf restoration effort needs all the help it can get.

CHAPTER 12

Agony in Alaska

It's difficult for non-Alaskans to understand Alaska. Twice the size of Texas, the state contains fewer people than Rhode Island. The eastern south-central region has a few roads, but the vast interior is essentially roadless, accessible mainly by airplane. So common and necessary are airplanes for travel in Alaska that the planes are billed as "air taxis."

Alaskans are different, too. Many moved to Alaska to get away from "civilization," and to live closer to wildlife. Alaskans typically have a strong attachment to the natural world, but are less sentimental and more utilitarian in their wildlife values than urbanized citizens of the lower 48.

Alaska also holds more wolves than any other state in the U.S., so it is hardly surprising—wolves being wolves, people being people—that Alaska also faces several major wolf management controversies. Some of the issues in the various wolf management debates are purely biological.

Others are primarily ethical or aesthetic. Most involve a queasy blend of hard science and personal choices, which is a classic recipe for disputes that generate more heat than light.

ANTECEDENTS

Wolves were once persecuted as vigorously in Alaska as they were elsewhere, although they were never close to being extirpated. The state simply contains too much land, too many wolves, and too few people to get the job done.

Before the general availability of airplanes following World War II, wolves in Alaska were usually trapped. After the war, people learned how effectively they could kill wolves from airplanes. A 1955 *Field & Stream* article, entitled "Strafing Arctic Killers," described the practice. In the story, the author congratulated himself for making more food available for Eskimo families by killing wolves. In the 1950s, federal authorities carried out a systematic anti-wolf

---

Wolves are relatively abundant in Alaska, yet management controversies abound.

program, using a combination of poison, traps, and gunners working from planes. A bounty encouraged private citizens to kill wolves.

Things changed in the 1960s, when state game agencies everywhere began hiring college graduates who had majored in the new science of game management. The new Alaska Department of Fish & Game (ADF&G), created when Alaska attained statehood in 1959, espoused a more modern and tolerant view of predators like wolves. The prevailing theory at the time held that the "balance of nature" prevented predators from harming prey populations. The ADF&G dropped the wolf bounty and reduced wolf control programs shortly after statehood. Wolves were reclassified as big game animals, and wolf numbers began to increase.

Then, in the late 1960s and early 1970s, some moose and caribou populations plummeted to desperately low levels, triggering general alarm. The crisis initiated a debate among Alaskans about what was wrong. Several factors were apparently responsible for the sharp decline in ungulate numbers. They included a succession of severe winters, heavy predation by wolves and bears, and excessive harvests by humans.

The great concern about ungulate populations coincided with the appearance of research from northeastern Minnesota and elsewhere suggesting that wolves could suppress ungulate populations under some circumstances. Researchers began to understand that wolf predation was not as benign as they had formerly believed.

ADF&G managers cut back on hunting of moose and caribou, and began reducing wolf numbers to let prey populations rebuild. The department also launched a series of research projects to study the complex web of predator-prey relationships. Several studies compared predator and prey populations in areas where wolves were controlled (by reducing their numbers) to areas where they were not controlled. In some study areas, the department wanted to remove a large percentage of the wolves in order to determine whether ungulate populations would benefit.

The announcement of that policy alarmed environmental groups. Alaska appeared to be returning to the old, discredited practice of killing wolves just when the rest of the nation was learning to appreciate them. People in the lower 48 were shocked to hear that hundreds of wolves—familiar to them as an endangered species—were being shot

each year in Alaska.

Meanwhile, results from a number of research projects convinced the ADF&G and a significant number of Alaskans that wolf control was an effective way of increasing depressed ungulate populations. With the exception of a small lunatic fringe, no Alaskans wanted wolves exterminated, but many believed it was necessary to decrease the wolf population in order to help moose and caribou recover.

Environmental groups didn't agree, and they began taking the department to court again and again. A bewildering and very expensive series of legal parries and feints followed every announced change in wolf management. As the contest wore on, each side became increasingly impatient with the opposition. Alaskans began to feel under siege from arrogant and uninformed outsiders who wanted to turn Alaska into "one big park." Environmental groups dis-

---

After World War II, Alaskans and visitors began hunting wolves from the air.

missed Alaskans as anachronistic wolf-haters with no ecological values. In an article in *Gray's Sporting Journal*, environmental writer Ted Williams sneered, "What is it with Alaskans? Is it simply that they tend to be more ignorant of ecology than the rest of us? Yes."

Just as truth is the first victim of war, credibility is an early victim of contentious resource management disputes. Rational debate becomes impossible when there is no agreement on basic facts.

A prime example is the disagreement about wolf numbers. Several environmental journalists claim that ADF&G's wolf managers have reduced wolf numbers from 10,000 in 1982 to 6,000 in just one decade. If true, this suggests that Alaska's wolves are headed toward extinction. ADF&G managers insist that statewide population estimates are a poor gauge of the status of wolves, because accurate surveys are available only from small portions of the state. Where managers have conducted

careful surveys, wolf populations have been steady or increasing. Moreover, the ADF&G contends that the earlier estimate of 10,000 wolves was "just a guess" that cannot fairly be compared to systematic surveys taken after 1984. According to the department, wolves occupy almost all of their traditional habitat, have recently extended their range, and are as plentiful as their food supply permits.

Who is right? Both the critics and the defenders of Alaska's wolf management include persuasive spokesmen with impressive credentials. Critics know that wildlife agencies can find ways to run studies so that the results support their management. Defenders of the ADF&G believe that critics prefer to stereotype Alaskans as anti-wolf, because that reduces a messy resource issue to a "good guys-bad guys" melodrama.

In disputes like this one, most people elect to believe the facts put forward by the group whose values they share. The arguments seem to be based on facts, but the facts may be arbitrarily chosen. At bottom, this kind of dispute is a clash of value systems.

A separate and equally contentious debate raged over "land-and-shoot" aerial hunting. The 1972 federal Airborne Hunting Act made it illegal to haze, herd, drive, harass, or shoot animals from airplanes. But it was still legal to spot a wolf or pack of wolves from the air, land a plane nearby, jump out, and shoot a wolf.

For many years, the ADF&G condoned land-and-shoot hunting. The practice offered recreation for some hunters and let the public help control wolf populations at little cost to taxpayers. Practically speaking, there is no effective way to hunt wolves in much of Alaska without using airplanes. Wolves are too elusive, and the country is too big. Land-and-shoot hunters harvested between 200 and 300 wolves annually in recent years.

But the practice has become extremely controversial. Critics began claiming that land-and-shoot hunters routinely broke the rules by shooting wolves from the air or hazing them to exhaustion before landing to finish them off. Since aerial hunting takes place in remote country with no witnesses, meaningful enforcement of the restrictions is difficult at best.

Land-and-shoot hunting might be practical, but the notion of hunting wolves from the air disgusted many people, including many hunters. Chasing and killing wolves from airplanes violates the principle of the "fair chase" and simply looks boorish

Some journalists claim that Alaska's wolf population has been reduced from 10,000 to 6,000 in just one decade.

and cruel. Land-and-shoot aerial hunting crystallized opposition to Alaska's wolf program in a way almost nothing could have, short of massive poisoning.

Nobody except the pilots and hunters involved will ever know how common the violations were. Eventually, a few violators were caught and tried. Critics felt that the court cases proved they had been right. The ADF&G claimed the same cases proved that the department had always been serious about enforcing the legal restrictions on land-and-shoot hunting.

Ultimately, negative publicity forced the ADF&G to alter its land-and-shoot policy. Land-and-shoot is no longer a usual and common hunting method. Yet the ADF&G refuses to give up on it altogether. It plans to allow private hunters to hunt wolves on a land-and-shoot basis by special permit. The ADF&G insists it will monitor the permits scrupulously, enforcing all regulations.

Fairly or unfairly, the land-and-shoot controversy gave the department a black eye by making it appear insensitive to ethical and aesthetic values. The controversy has not altogether disappeared with the cessation (which might be temporary) of the practice.

For all the furor it caused, land-and-shoot has been a side issue. The heart of the Alaskan wolf controversy involves disagreement over the legitimacy of controlling—that is, killing—wolves as a regular method of managing moose and caribou. The issue raises a number of serious questions, and the answers are not simple. They depend on research findings that often (but not exclusively) come from the ADF&G, which means that skeptical critics dismiss them. Yet the questions are worth pursuing. If nothing else, the effort illustrates the hazards of summing up wildlife management with simple axioms.

Perhaps the most efficient way to attack the complex issue is through a series of questions and answers:

Do Alaskans hate wolves?

A few do. But many Alaskans revere wolves, and the great majority seem to feel that wolves are an important part of the state's wildlife resources. Perhaps the only neutral authority on this question is Yale's Steven Kellert, a researcher who has conducted extensive surveys of American attitudes toward wolves. In a 1985 survey, Kellert identified Alaskans as one of the two demographic groups with the greatest affection for wolves.

How many wolves are killed in

Alaska each year?

The total legal annual kill has ranged between 700 and 900 recently. The annual harvest is about 11 to 14 percent of the state's wolf population.

Is the ADF&G scapegoating the wolf in order to let humans kill more moose and caribou than they should?

According to ADF&G data, people kill only one to five percent of the ungulates, whereas predators take about 25 percent. Predators are thus taking at least five times as many moose and caribou as human hunters.

Alaska's ungulates are under significant pressure. Research shows that when the combined mortality from weather, hunting, and predation exceeds 20 to 30 percent, ungulate populations can get stuck at low levels ("low" is defined as numbers significantly less than the habitat could support).

Is there any way of controlling wolf populations without shooting or trapping them?

Not yet, although some researchers are investigating the possibility of

---

A 1985 survey indicated that Alaskans have great affection for wolves.

reducing wolf populations through birth control. There is currently no wolf birth control technique (other than surgical alteration) that does not have side effects. This will be an active area of research in the future.

Research shows that it might be possible to reduce grizzly and wolf predation on moose calves by dropping the carcasses of road-killed moose in selected areas at times when the young calves are most vulnerable. But this "diversionary feeding" technique is prohibitively expensive in a large, virtually roadless state like Alaska.

Can ungulate populations be increased without controlling predation at all?

Some managers believe intensive habitat manipulation (such as rejuvenating old brush with controlled burning) offers the hope of boosting moose numbers. The feasibility and cost of this sort of management have not yet been fully assessed.

Adjusting the human harvest also affects ungulate populations, but to a limited degree. Since predators take at least five times as many ungulates as humans, the gains to be realized by reducing the human harvest are limited.

Is the ADF&G selling out to commercial hunting interests, killing wolves to maximize the money that the state receives from sport hunting?

There is an economic incentive for the ADF&G to manage for increased ungulate harvests. Each non-resident moose hunter leaves about $6,000 in the state's economy. That money is appreciated in Alaska, as it would be in any other state. Many industries, such as farming and manufacturing, are incompatible with Alaska's geography and remote location. The state has traditionally seen its natural resources as a legitimate source of income. Yet this does not prove that Alaska's ungulate management is biased by a desire to profit from the guided hunt industry.

Dick Bishop is a retired biologist active in Alaskan conservation causes. "I've attended umpty-ump resource meetings all over the state," Bishop says. "They showed me that the economic motive is not uppermost in the minds of most Alaskans. What matters to Alaskans is the opportunity to hunt for their own meat. People have strong feelings about that. I find it interesting that outsiders acknowledge that native hunters have spiritual and cultural reasons for hunting, while denying that the same factors could motivate white Alaskans. They do."

Minnesota's deer herd is booming

while wolves enjoy full protection. Why would producing high ungulate populations in Alaska require wolf control when it's not required in Minnesota?

First, we shouldn't assume that Minnesota's wolves have totally escaped "control." A few wolves are killed each year by depredation program agents, and many more are killed illegally. Although it is difficult to determine the extent of the illegal kill, the number is significant. In other words, Minnesota is not a pure example of a predator-prey system operating with no human-caused mortality.

Moreover, Minnesota has been lucky in recent years. In the early years of the state's revamped deer management, harsh winters and wolf predation suppressed deer numbers in northeastern Minnesota. Wolves and deer have flourished side-by-side in Minnesota for only about a decade, a decade of atypically benign winters. It is too early to cite Minnesota as a model of how wolves and whitetails interrelate.

Finally, managers caution against applying the lessons of one predator-prey system to another. Minnesota has a wolf-deer system, with other prey species playing a minor role. Alaska has various combinations of wolves, grizzly bears, and black bears preying on various combinations of caribou, moose, sheep, and other prey species.

Why does that make a difference?

Some classic studies of predator-prey relations featuring wolves as the main predator (such as the Isle Royale moose-wolf study) have involved simple systems with one or two prey species and one predator. Less is known about more complex systems such as Alaska's and Canada's, where caribou and moose suffer significant predation from humans, grizzly bears, and wolves.

In particular, research shows that the combined predation of grizzly bears and wolves on moose (especially very young moose) can suppress moose numbers.

If grizzly bears play a major role in hurting ungulate populations, why shouldn't grizzlies be controlled just as wolves are in order to increase ungulate numbers?

Alaska's predator control focuses on the wolf rather than the grizzly for several reasons.

The grizzly is a long-lived species with low fertility. Wolves, on the other hand, are so productive that they can sustain high annual mortality. In Alaska, it's possible to kill 30 to 40 percent of the wolves in a region every year without reducing overall

wolf numbers. Regions that lose too many wolves are restocked by dispersing wolves from adjacent packs. Mistakes in wolf control have only temporary effects, because the wolf is a more resilient, fertile, and mobile species than the grizzly.

Moreover, there are ways to manage grizzlies without resorting to major predator control programs. Grizzlies are less elusive than wolves. They can be hunted in traditional ways without using airplanes. Thus grizzly numbers are managed through the common wildlife management technique of a limited sport hunting harvest.

Wolves are generally thought to prey on the young, old, sick, and unfit ungulates. How can wolves hurt moose and caribou populations when their predation is mainly directed at vulnerable animals?

ADF&G managers argue that their critics rely too much on old research suggesting that predation is benign, while ignoring many studies indicating that wolf predation can damage ungulate populations. In a balanced predator-prey system, wolves do selectively hunt vulnerable animals. When ungulate populations fail, though, wolves are forced to hunt healthier animals. Alaska's wolf managers claim that wolves are more capable of catching healthy adult prey than wolf fans in the lower 48 usually believe.

A number of studies in Alaska and the Yukon have documented the dangers of heavy predation on young ungulates. If predators kill over 90 percent of the caribou calves—as they did in some studies—caribou numbers are pinned at low levels. Moose are even more vulnerable. Typically, 100 cow moose give birth to about 120 to 140 calves each year. In some studies, predators whittled that group to just 10 to 20 survivors at summer's end. Moose cannot sustain population levels while losing 90 percent of their young each year.

The issue is complex, and the research does not point in one direction. Caribou seem better able than moose to rebound from population lows, apparently because they migrate. Still, the weight of research from Alaska and the Yukon suggests that heavy predation on young ungulates can prevent a distressed population from rebuilding to the level the habitat should be able to sustain.

Why doesn't the "balance of nature" principle work in Alaska? If ungulate populations crash, wolf populations will simply follow. Why should it be necessary to manipulate wolf populations?

The balance of nature principle does work in Alaska. But it doesn't work the way people think it does, in Alaska or elsewhere.

The correlation between prey and predator species numbers is not entirely neat and predictable. Several studies in Alaska and Canada indicate that when a prey population gets in trouble, predator populations don't automatically plummet. Bears, because they are omnivores, switch diets when one food source becomes scarce. Similarly, wolves are resourceful enough to scratch out a living for some time when their preferred food source dries up.

It isn't easy. Pup mortality and pack-to-pack aggression increase. But the adult wolves carry on. Ultimately, when their main prey species hits hard times, so do wolves. But "ultimately" can take a long time. According to some studies, there may be a time lag of up to several decades before predator numbers strike a new balance with prey numbers.

Why not simply let predator and prey numbers seek their own level?

Some studies in Alaska and northwestern Canada suggest that the "normal" or "natural" situation is a balance between very low prey and very low predator numbers. In those circumstances, predator and prey species are in no threat of extinction, but both exist at low levels.

Another outcome is possible, an outcome that seems much more attractive to many Alaskans. Studies have shown that manipulating wolf numbers can allow moose to rebound. By interfering in this way, managers can create a different predator-prey balance, one that features strong numbers of both moose and wolves.

The goal seems desirable: a balanced predator-prey system with high wolf numbers and enough moose to enable Alaska's white and native hunters to enjoy successful fall hunts. The "catch" is that the only feasible way to achieve that goal is by removing significant numbers of wolves through trapping or aerial shooting.

ZONED MANAGEMENT

The ADF&G is currently implementing a zoned management program for wolves and ungulates. Zone 1 lands will be regarded as "let nature take its course" regions in which wolves will be fully protected. Zone 7 lands will feature intensive management (including wolf control) to produce high numbers of wolves and ungulates. Other zones will be intermediate in terms of how much wolf control and habitat management they receive.

Zoned management makes excellent sense, and is the way big game populations are managed by progressive state wildlife agencies. But that doesn't mean there's an end in sight to the Alaskan wolf management controversy. Some Alaskans and non-resident hunters will continue to feel that the state has too many wolves and not enough moose and caribou. Some fans of wolves, both within and outside of the state, will be distressed because they believe that too much land is designated for wolf control.

The ADF&G is currently trying to assess the preferences of the public, so it can adjust the zones and provide the appropriate management. However, "the public" doesn't exist. Instead, there are several diverse publics, local and national, some of which have wildly divergent visions of wolf management. Even if you ignore the most extreme positions on this controversy, several issues remain about which reasonable people can disagree. And they do.

According to Bob Stephenson, a biologist and manager with the ADF&G, "With so many competing political pressures on our wolf management, there is a sort of balance that limits our options. For example, if some state politician directed us to eliminate a bunch of wolves, we couldn't, because we'd get absolutely killed by both the national press and many groups in Alaska."

Weeks after Stephenson spoke, the ADF&G did indeed get "killed" by the national press. As the department worked to implement its zoned management program, it tentatively decided to increase moose and caribou numbers in the Forty-mile and Delta Control Areas by reducing wolf populations. Wolf numbers would eventually return to previous levels in the Delta area and would increase in the Forty-mile area.

When details of the plan reached the press, reporters set news wires humming. The stories that emerged rarely mentioned the purpose of the plan and failed to place the ADF&G proposed wolf control measures in the context of Alaska's overall wolf management plans. The main point made by the news stories was that Alaska was about to kill great numbers of wolves from helicopter gunships.

The public response was quick and almost uniformly negative. Pro-wolf and environmental groups called for a boycott on Alaska tourism. Many groups cancelled plans to hold conventions in the state. Hostile phone calls and letters were received from all around the U.S. and even from fans of wolves in other nations.

Tourism, Alaska's third-largest industry, was badly jeopardized. Faced with a public relations disaster, Governor Walter Hickle announced that the state would delay its implementation of the plan until a summit conference on wolf management was held.

The three-day summit happened in early 1993. According to one participant, "It was like forcing dialogue between pro-life and pro-choice folks, and I'm afraid very few minds were changed." When the summit concluded, managers were left with the task of seeking compromise management programs that might be acceptable to groups adhering to irreconcilably different philosophies.

Alaska's wolf management program proceeds daily under a harsh spotlight of national and international scrutiny. Different groups continue to lobby for different management goals, and the debate shows no signs of becoming more relaxed or rational. Increasingly, the only acceptable management option to many fans of wolves is a strict "don't tinker with Mother Nature" program. It remains to be seen whether pro-wolf public opinion, much of it coming from outside of Alaska, will dictate the direction of the state's wolf management.

CHAPTER 13

The Future of the Wolf

Prospects for wolf restoration are brighter now than they were a few decades ago—or even one decade ago. Public attitudes toward wolves are changing from hatred to adoration at bewildering speed. Fans of wolves might conclude that the battle for acceptance of the wolf has been won.

It has not. While support for wolves today appears to be broad, it is almost certainly not as deep as it seems. All surveys indicate general public support for wolf restoration. But that support can melt when wolves cause problems for people. Public opinion surveys never ask such questions as: "Do you want wolves restored in your area, even if they will occasionally kill someone's pet?" So far, wolf restoration has involved negligible human sacrifices. We will know more about this tolerance of wolves when people are asked to put the welfare of wolves above their own interests in some significant way.

If wolves were more delicate, the social cost of bringing them back would be higher. Fortunately, the wolf is a remarkable animal that doesn't require coddling. This in turn means that people won't have to make great sacrifices in order to allow wolves to establish viable populations. Still, some sacrifices will be necessary.

ROADS OR WOLVES?

Roads and wolves do not mix happily. For example, Wisconsin's Highway 13, along which my family has spotted wolves on two occasions, is currently being upgraded. We travel slowly when driving 13 at night. In places, timber and brush crowd the asphalt so tightly that deer can appear with no warning whatsoever. Upgraded, brush-free portions of 13 encourage traffic to move briskly. The improved highway will surely attract more vehicles, making it more of a barrier and a threat to wolves than the old highway.

Improving one highway will not

The wolf's prospects are brighter now than they were a decade ago, but the battle for wolf restoration has not been won.

doom the wolf in northern Wisconsin, but the issue isn't one highway. Unless people change priorities, we will someday upgrade one highway too many, making northern Wisconsin that much more convenient for automobiles and that much less suitable for wolves. Wolves would benefit if every upgraded highway were balanced by one that is downgraded—a "no net upgrade" highway policy—but that seems unlikely.

Wolves require sizable tracts of unsettled land. Suitable habitat still exists in the Great Lakes states and the northern Rockies. But human populations continue to increase, as does human pressure for access to wild land. Even if future generations regard the animals highly, wolves will be threatened as human development chips away at the diminishing supply of wild lands. In the past, wolves suffered directly because people killed

Above, a manager tranquilizes a timber wolf in northern Wisconsin.

them at every opportunity. In the future, wolves will suffer indirectly because well-intentioned people—wildlife-loving people like my own family—want to live in wild country.

Every time a family like mine builds a wilderness cabin retreat, we motivate the local community to upgrade roads, to improve services, and to develop more acres of wild lands to pay for all that. The process is hard to see, because it involves so many tiny changes and because it moves with the slow, inexorable speed of a glacier. The net effect, though, is the suburbanization of the last wild lands in America. Wolves cannot, will not, and should not live in suburbia.

Ongoing development is another reason to move forward with wolf restoration at full speed. We have a good opportunity now to restore a magnificent animal to representative blocks of its original habitat in the Great Lakes states, the northern Rockies, and the Southwest. Finding living space for wolves will be more difficult in the twenty-first century.

THE NEED FOR UNDERSTANDING

While wolf restoration can almost be considered successfully concluded in the Upper Midwest, much work lies ahead in the West. In terms of sheer voting power, wolf advocates are probably in a position to impose wolf restoration despite adamant resistance from cattlemen, wool growers, and hunting outfitters. However, to do so would be foolish. In the words of a Wisconsin manager, "This is not an animal you can force down people's throats."

The need for consensus doesn't mean that wolf advocates should accept the agonizingly slow pace at which wolf restoration has been moving in the West. The most effective course of action would combine public education on wolves, sustained pressure for restoration, and reasonable accommodation of the concerns of people who fear wolves.

The only responsible position for wolf advocates is to endorse carefully designed and fully funded livestock depredation programs. Wolf restoration cannot succeed if the people who live closest to wolves suffer financially. The general public wants wolves returned to the West. The general public owes it to cattle and sheep producers to ensure that the inevitable losses, however small, are not borne exclusively by ranchers. Ranchers deserve a program that quickly removes the few wolves that acquire the habit of attacking livestock. The need for a good depredation program is accepted by wildlife managers, researchers like Dave Mech, and an increasing number of wolf advocacy groups, particularly the Defenders of Wildlife. This is not an "anti-wolf" stance.

The future of America's two most endangered wolves, the red wolf and the Mexican wolf, depends almost entirely on funding. Both the funding and the continued existence of the red wolf seem reasonably secure. In spite of federal budget problems, money must be found to set the Mexican wolf program firmly on its feet.

As Alaska moves to zoned wolf management, the primary dispute lies in determining which lands should be zoned to receive wolf control and which should not. This is a genuine resource management issue about which reasonable public debate is desirable. But name-calling and mutual distrust have poisoned the discussion. The debate must be conducted with more civility and mutual respect.

THE ESA

The fate of the northern Rocky mountain wolf and the Mexican wolf depends on renewal of the Endangered Species Act (ESA). The ESA is popu-lar, yet vulnerable. Extremely powerful forces, often disguised as conservation groups, are organizing to destroy or weaken it.

The ESA is a curious law with several flaws that conservationists are reluctant to admit in public. The law is rigid and costly. Some of its provisions are vague, while others are contradictory. The ESA often gives a failing species no support until it is sick unto death, at which point the law suddenly mandates expensive emergency measures. Its focus on species instead of critical habitats is considered a mistake by many conservationists.

But if the ESA is a crude tool, it is also one of the most powerful laws ever written for preventing great ecological harm. The law even has some power to correct past mistakes, which is rare; most conservation bills limit only the amount or rate of environmental degradation. Environmentalists shudder when contemplating what would happen to their ability to affect public policy if the ESA were gutted.

In particular, the ESA is critically important for the future of wolves and countless other species. It must be renewed. Perhaps when that is done, the act can be made a little less threatening to people who live near the critical habitat of endangered species.

The renewal of the ESA is critical, but nothing is more important to the wolf's future than public education.

TOWARD BALANCE

Nothing is more important to the future of wolves than public education. In this sense, time is on the side of wolves. The most antagonistic opponents of wolves, according to Yale researcher Steven Kellert, are older people living in sparsely populated rural areas. Though it sounds unkind to say so, their wolf hatred will be buried with them in the next few decades. Meanwhile, many youngsters reared on Julie of the Wolves (written in 1972) are now voting adults. And they don't just tolerate wolves—they adore wolves.

There is a danger in their adoration. As public opinion swings back and forth on any topic, it continually overcompensates. Much of today's literature on wolves idealizes and ascribes lofty human qualities to them. The guilt that American society feels about centuries of wolf hatred, commendable and appropriate as it is, has led us to romanticize the

wolf—a harmless error, were it not for the way that wolf worship can interfere with responsible wolf management.

Dick Thiel, a former wolf manager for Wisconsin, speaks for many managers when he says, "Frankly, this animal is messy. You put it too close to people and you occasionally get trouble. The lovey-dovey types who support these critters are going to have to accept that there are places where wolves should not exist, because they are too close to people. And the public needs to learn to trust resource managers to determine how wolves are managed."

The problem is real. Wildlife managers have long been second-guessed by sportsmen who think they know more than "so-called experts with college degrees." Increasingly, wolf advocates who are suspicious of the motives of today's managers are making it difficult for the managers to do their jobs. Some fans of wolves oppose any form of wolf management except total protection. Dedicated wolf managers today often have to fight a war on two fronts, defending their policies against wolf-haters and wolf-lovers alike. Most wolf managers deserve more trust and support than they receive.

VOICES FOR WISE MANAGEMENT

One of the most promising developments for the wolf's long-range future is the creation of several institutions dedicated to educating the public.

One of the newest is the International Wolf Center (IWC) in Ely, Minnesota. The IWC is constructing a modern facility that will showcase wolf educational materials. Most prominent among them will be the influential, award-winning "Wolves & Humans" exhibit created in 1983 by the Science Museum of Minnesota. The new IWC building opens to the public in July, 1993. A resident pack of captive wolves will be on view, adding beauty and drama to the experience that people have when they tour the indoor exhibits.

An organization like this was badly needed. The IWC is a non-profit organization whose mission is to serve as a focal point for worldwide environmental education about the wolf, the wolf's relationship with other species, and the role of the wolf within human cultures. The IWC is not an advocacy group, but a fair-minded and scientifically responsible educational organization. Most of the time, efforts to educate the public about wolves concentrate on dispelling old negative stereotypes. Yet there is a difference between education and advocacy.

The IWC offers many experiential programs in wolf country. These include field trips, research expeditions, howling expeditions, and other activities that allow people to learn more about wolves. Some of the center's programs are run cooperatively with Vermillion Community College and offer college credit to successful participants. The IWC's outreach programs include a speaker's bureau that is active in Minnesota and other states. IWC members receive *International Wolf*, a quarterly journal that is a superb source of current news on wolf research and wolf management controversies. Anyone interested in wolves will be richly rewarded for the $25 investment in an individual ("Lone Wolf") membership or a $50 family ("Wolf Pack") membership. The addresses of wolf organizations and political groups appear in Appendix II.

Similar activities take place at Wolf Park, a non-profit organization in Battle Ground, Indiana. Wolf Park maintains about 20 wolves in an enclosure with a herd of buffalo. To the greatest degree possible, the wolves live in conditions that approximate life in the wild, although they are fed deer and cow carcasses and are not allowed to prey on the bison.

Wolf Park sponsors a variety of research and educational programs. Seminars, howling sessions, internships, and other programs offer educational opportunities and contact with wolves. The park is open weekend afternoons from May through November. It is particularly important that an institution like this exists in the eastern half of the continent, because most wolf-viewing opportunities are limited to the western U.S.

Wolf Park produces a quarterly publication called WOLF! It is a good-sized publication (a recent issue had 64 pages) that carefully tracks all the unfolding national and international issues related to wolf management. A subscription costs $18.50 per year.

Wolf Haven International, in Tenino, Washington, is also a nonprofit organization working for wolf conservation. The group's international membership exceeds 14,000. Wolf Haven's newsletter alerts members to conservation issues and presents current thinking on wolves and wolf management. The group helps fund various wolf management projects, such as surveys of wolves in northwestern states, where they are beginning to recolonize old habitat. Wolf Haven maintains a sanctuary for wolves, with several dozen wolves held in enclosures that are as natural as possible. Guided tours of the sanctuary are available on request. Some of the refuge wolves are occasionally taken to schools to serve as ambassadors for their species. Individual memberships cost $25 per year.

A new group has been created to teach Alaskans and Alaska's many tourists about wolves. Wolf Song of Alaska is a private, non-profit organization with a purely educational mission. Based in Anchorage, Wolf Song is currently raising funds to create a multi-million dollar facility of 300 to 500 acres, which will include a resident pack of wolves. Wolf Song has its own wolf educational display and has hosted the award-winning "Wolves & Humans" exhibit. Membership costs $25 annually, and Wolf Song publishes a newsletter.

Many other organizations work for wolves through political influence and legal actions. Nationally, the most prominent groups have been the Sierra Club, the Audubon Society, and Defenders of Wildlife. All have been concerned and influential, although some observers believe these groups have at times been overly protectionist. Defenders of Wildlife has evolved from its early protectionist perspective toward a more comprehensive stance that tries to respectfully consider the concerns of wolf opponents.

To depolarize arguments on wolf restoration in the Rockies and the Southwest, Defenders has created a fund to compensate ranchers who have lost livestock to wolf depredation. Sportsmen have long been willing to pay for programs that support game animals. Oddly enough, the so-called "non-consumptive" fans of wildlife have traditionally been reluctant to open their checkbooks in order to support the wildlife management programs they advocate. Defenders is a refreshing exception. The group puts out a hotline publication, *Wolf Action*, that keeps members abreast of the latest twists in the legal battles over wolf restoration.

The Wolf Fund is a single-issue organization. It exists solely to restore wolves to Yellowstone, and will probably disappear the moment that objective has been accomplished. The group's founder, Renee Askins, has been recognized nationally as a particularly effective representative for wolves. The Wolf Fund members fervently believe that wolves belong in Yellowstone. Acknowledging that some wolves are likely to stray from the park and cause problems, the Wolf Fund endorses prudent depredation control measures.

The Wolf Fund is supported by foundations and private donors. There is no membership fee. Anyone sharing an interest in the Yellowstone wolf controversy can receive the organization's newsletter, a literate and attractive publication that strives to appear twice a year.

Because the Mexican wolf restoration program is under-funded, the important work of public education is being borne on the surprisingly muscular shoulders of volunteer committees in Arizona, New Mexico, and Texas. The committees conduct programs in schools, donate money to depredation compensation programs, meet with livestock industry groups, and conduct surveys on wolf attitudes. The Arizona group, Preserve Arizona's Wolves (P.A.W.S.), is currently trying to raise money to improve captive-breeding facilities.

THE SECOND CHANCE

While my work on this book has convinced me that it is dangerous to

reduce wolves to symbols, I believe the restoration of wolves will be one of the major symbolic events in human history. As a species, humans have been violent, greedy, and short-sighted. Humans in general—and Americans in particular—have abused wolves. We owe it to the wolf to try one more time to work out a relationship that protects legitimate human interests while allowing living space for wolves.

Further, I would argue, we owe it to ourselves to try again to manage wolves wisely. When Americans learn to tolerate and respect wolves, we will have exorcised something sin-gularly ugly in our national character.

The true measure of the morality of a political society is how justly it treats its least powerful and popular citizens. In much the same sense, the ecological decency of a society can be measured by how it treats the most troublesome and notorious animal species. When our society proves it has learned to live with wolves, we can begin to like ourselves a little better. It will then be time to ponder how we can improve our relations with several hundred other species, but not before pausing to celebrate the extraordinary progress represented by the return of the wolf.

When our society has learned to live with wolves, we can begin to like ourselves a little better.

Appendix I
More About Wolves

This book introduces readers to certain issues about the lives of wolves, the history of human attitudes toward wolves, and wolf management. Readers should understand that most of the topics raised in the book are much more complcated than I have been able to indicate. Every chapter is worthy subject matter for a whole book, and in several cases whole books have been written about topics that I could only discuss briefly. In short, I urge the reader to explore the fascinating world of wolves further through additional reading.

There are two fine introductory level books. Both offer a generous number of attractive photographs. Dave Mech's *The Way of the Wolf* sums up a lifetime of research in language that any adult and many children can understand. Mech is not only the world's foremost authority on wolves but a good writer who is always clear and interesting. Candace Savage's *Wolves* covers much of the same material. Savage's book has richer photographic support but less text than Mech's.

Readers who want more depth should read Mech's classic *The Wolf*. Although it was not written for a popular audience, the prose is readable and not overly technical. This book sums up scholarly knowledge of wolves as of 1970. While I researched *The Return of the Wolf*, I referred to *The Wolf* as "the bible." I later learned that wolf students around the world call it by the same name. Unlike the better-known Bible, however, this one could use an update. A great deal of research has been done in the past two decades. But *The Wolf* has aged well, and in the process has done an enormous amount of good for enlightened wolf management.

Of Wolves and Men, written by Barry Lopez, became an instant classic in nature writing when it appeared in 1978. Lopez deals quickly with basic facts about wolves, then sets sail across the previously uncharted waters of man's obsessive hatred of wolves. It is absorbing (although saddening) reading. Lopez occasionally crosses the line into mysticism, as when he suggests that a prey animal gives permission for wolves to take its life, but his writing is intelligent and his topic deeply moving.

Three books have resulted from the remarkable encounter between Mech, Jim Brandenburg, and the wolves of Ellesmere Island. Each man has published a book about the experience of sharing the lives of arctic wolves. Mech's *The Arctic Wolf, Living With the Pack*, is stronger on biological observations. Brandenburg might be the world's most accomplished wolf photographer. His *White Wolf* is quite readable and contains some stunningly beautiful photographs. Mech has just published *Wolves of the High Arctic*, summing up five years of continuous contact with the pack. His experience marks the first time that a trained observer has been able to watch individual wolves grow up and assume different roles within a pack.

Anyone interested in the personal experience of conducting wolf research might enjoy Roger Peters' well-written *Dance of the Wolves*. The book is a novelized depiction of Peters' work as a research assistant. The identities of people and places in the book have been changed . . . although not to such a degree that they can't be identified by anyone who's strongly interested.

Canadian writer R.D. Lawrence has won a following for his nature writing, particularly his work on wolves. His *In Praise of Wolves* is most interesting for its careful description of the complexities of communication between people and wolves in confinement. I find Lawrence a bit opinionated, but his insights have benefited legions of readers.

Two of the old classics are timeless in their appeal. Adolph Murie's *The Wolves of Mount McKinley* is still being studied and enjoyed by students of wolves. It's hard to grant enough credit to Murie for his energy, patience, and honesty. Lois Crisler's *Arctic Wild* is more uneven, but probably more fascinating. If Crisler's prose sometimes wanders, she nonetheless creates striking lines that ring like chimes. Crisler had the privilege of living intimately with wolves, an experience that few humans can (or should) have. Both books were wonderfully original in their time, and both make rewarding reading today.

Jan DeBlieu's *Meant to Be Wild* tells the story of efforts to save endangered species through captive breeding programs. About a third of the text is devoted to the red wolf program, and it's enthralling reading. DeBlieu's account of the red wolf program is rich in the human drama that gets excluded from official descriptions of federal management programs. For example, she describes the tragi-comedy of researchers chasing a wayward wolf around a trailer park, desperately trying to capture the animal before it could create "an incident." DeBlieu has the right amount of respect for science and the ethical sensitivity to see both the promise and hazards of captive breeding programs.

Unfortunately, no book of comparable quality exists about the lobo. *Vanishing Lobo*, by newspaper writer James C. Burbank, is a disappointment. It's mostly a fuzzy reworking of themes developed more effectively by Lopez. *The Wolf In the Southwest*, edited by David E. Brown, is primarily a historical account of the great campaign to extirpate the Mexican wolf. Much of the material comes from the accounts of federal wolf trappers—a group known for self-aggrandizing exaggeration.

Only one modern book deals with the northern Rocky Mountain wolf. While Rick Bass's *The Ninemile Wolves* is limited in scope, it's one of the best books written about wolves. Bass mainly tells the story of the wolves that recently began showing up in Montana's Ninemile Valley. He's a poet with strong feelings about his subject: "They say not to anthropomorphize—and I'm learning not to—but in some respects, it seems bend-over-backwards ridiculous *not* to,

for if a wolf does not have a spirit, then what animal, including ourselves, can be said to have one?" Bass is heady stuff. After reading him, you might want to sober up with a chapter or two of Mech.

The books mentioned above are generally not appropriate for children, although an adult could read selectively from Mech's *The Way of the Wolf* and point out the significance of the photos. Several outstanding wolf books have been written for children. The *Wolves* volume in the Zoobooks series is illustrated with colorful paintings that help children understand how wolves live. *The Wonder of Wolves,* by Sandra Chisholm Robinson, combines text and art with a number of activities (games, crossword puzzles, art projects) that make wolf education fun. Tom Wolpert's *Wolves for Kids* offers a goodly helping of useful natural history information and is illustrated with striking photographs.

Two soft-bound brochures explain the issues relevant to wolf recovery in the northern Rockies. The Wildlife Management Institute offers a balanced, understandable 20-page brochure called *Wolves in the Northern Rockies.* The National Audubon Society and the National Fish and Wildlife Foundation co-sponsored a 32-page brochure that not only covers the northern Rockies and Yellowstone, but presents a great deal of information about wolves in general. The brochure, entitled *Wolf Recovery in the Northern Rocky Mountains*, was written by Whitney Tilt, Ruth Norris, and Amos S. Eno. It's a valuable resource.

The Timber Wolf Alliance, a group associated with the Sigurd Olson Environmental Institute, sells a resource directory called *Beyond Little Red Riding Hood.* The directory lists materials available for those who want to know more about wolves—including books, audio and video tapes, curriculum guides, booklets, tape shows, and wolf organizations. While anyone may find this directory interesting, it's especially valuable for teachers who are organizing a curriculum unit on wolves.

Appendix II
Selected Wolf Groups

Below is a list of groups working for wolf restoration or better wolf manage-ment. There are many other wolf groups, and new ones are constantly being organized. The associations listed here have been recommended by people familiar with wolf management controversies.

Canadian Wolf Defenders
Box 3480, Station D, Edmonton, Alberta, Canada T5L 4J3
Defenders of Wildlife
1244 19th St. N.W., Washington, DC 20036
International Wolf Center
1396 Highway 169, Ely, MN 55731
Mexican Wolf Coalition of New Mexico
Carol Martindale, 7239 Esleta Blvd. S.W., Albuquerque, NM 87105
Mexican Wolf Coalition of Texas
Marcia Sullivan, 5815 Crooked Post, Spring, TX 77383
National Audubon Society
801 Pennsylvania Ave. S.E., Washington, DC 20003
National Wildlife Federation
1400 16th St NW, Washington, DC 20036-2266
North American Wolf Society
Box 82950, Fairbanks, AK 99708
Northwest Wildlife Preservation Society
Box 34129, Station "D", Vancouver, British Columbia, Canada V6J 4N3
P.A.W.S. (Preserve Arizona's Wolves)
Bobbie Holaday 1413 East Dobbins Rd., Phoenix, AZ 85040
Sierra Club
730 Polk St., San Francisco, CA 94109
Timber Wolf Alliance
Sigurd Olson Environmental Institute, Northland College, Ashland, WI 54806
Wolf Fund
Center for the Humanities and the Environment, Box 471, Moose, WY 83012
Wolf Haven International
3111 Offut Lake Rd., Tenino, WA 98589
Wolf Park
North American Wildlife Park Foundation, Battle Ground, IN 47920
Wolf Recovery Foundation
Box 793, Boise, ID 83701
Wolf Song of Alaska
Box 110309, Anchorage, AK 99511-0309